POEMS THAT INSPIRE YOU TO THINK AND GROW RICH

POEMS THAT INSPIRE YOU TO THINK AND GROW RICH

Napoleon Hill

COMPILED WITH COMMENTARY BY

Judith Williamson

An Approved Publication of The Napoleon Hill Foundation

MEDIA

Published 2019 by Gildan Media LLC
aka G&D Media
www.GandDmedia.com

Front Cover design by David Rheinhardt of Pyrographx

Interior design by Meghan Day Healey of Story Horse, LLC

Library of Congress Cataloging-in-Publication Data is available upon request

ISBN: 978-1-7225-0119-8

10   9   8   7   6   5   4   3   2   1

Whatever the mind can conceive and believe, the mind can achieve.

—NAPOLEON HILL

CONTENTS

FOREWORD

This book of inspirational poems is intended to focus the reader on personal success. Igniting a burning fire of enthusiasm under one's definite major purpose is the method Dr. Hill suggests for getting your life's purpose off the ground. Poetry is well known for emotionalizing a subject. Topics such as purpose, applied faith, personal initiative and others are aligned with poems and commentary intended to raise your level of enthusiasm. As you respond to this call, your own life's purpose will rise to the top of your awareness. Then as you reflect on the poems, you can begin to address personal issues that may have blocked or even stopped your attainment of your life's purpose in the past.

Poetry changes your level of awareness. It is like having your eyes dilated. You are still looking out through the same set of eyes, but you are seeing things differently.

Poetry causes us to change our lens of awareness and to look through another's eyes, or to see another's viewpoint. Seeing another's point of view can provide us with options that we did not even know we had.

One of my favorite poetic pieces is a stanza from "Auguries of Innocence" by William Blake. It reads:

To see a World in a Grain of Sand
And a Heaven in a Wild Flower
Hold Infinity in the palm of your hand
And Eternity in an hour.

As you can imagine, these short four lines hold many messages. To me they say such things as: look within, appreciate small beauties, everything is important, and beauty is all around us. And, understood is the message that all our worlds are significant and we can each experience multiple and simultaneously different realities. A short life is as meaningful as one lasting a century. It all comes down to how you view it.

So much potential for interpretation is packed into the above four short lines of poetry. As we meditate on the meanings of the lines, we cannot but help expand our personal awareness of life as well. Poems enable us to grow beyond the written page and to traverse unknown territories without even leaving our armchair.

How can one argue that poems are superficial and perhaps only cute little ditties for grandparents to read to their grandchildren? Rather, they are for each of us and serve as daily enrichment, daily success vitamins as Dr. Hill would say, for our spiritual selves. Try a few a day, and ask yourself in a week or two whether or not you are feeling more inspired? I think you will be surprised at how you can control your enthusiasm at will. Remember, "Whatever the mind can conceive and believe, it can achieve."

—Judith Williamson

INTRODUCTION

This book of poems is compiled to inspire the reader to *Think and Grow Rich*. Poetry is an art form that oftentimes can be difficult for modern day readers to interpret. However, the 101 poems contained in this volume have been individually selected to speak directly to the heart in simple language that is easily understood by most everyone.

Poems by their very nature are compressed thought that is highly emotional. When you are attempting to succeed in any project or purpose, emotionalizing yourself for success—reaching the white heat of a burning desire—moves you toward your goal in a quicker fashion. Poetry offers us the emotionalism that can supercharge our purpose.

Whether you lack courage, drive, cheerfulness, confidence, determination, or simply need the shot in the arm that poems can give you, this book will speak personally to you.

Perhaps you will recall a line that you have memorized from a favorite poem, and now you have found the entire poem. Perhaps you have often heard a phrase recited as a maxim, and have wondered about its source. Perhaps a line jumps out at you and burns its way into your memory and you repeat it again and again like the line from a favorite song. Perhaps this collection of inspirational poetry will do what some of the pieces did for Napoleon Hill—inspire you to *Think and Grow Rich*.

In addition to the poems themselves, this little anthology offers vintage commentary by Napoleon Hill in order to help you understand the significance of the sections. The book is divided into eleven sections that include: definiteness of purpose, applied faith, going the extra mile, personal initiative, positive mental attitude, self-discipline, accurate thinking, teamwork, adversity and defeat, and cosmic habitforce. Students of Dr. Hill will recognize these as 10 of the 17 principles of the Science of Success. The names have been left as they appear in the course although other names for the categories are interchangeable. For example, teamwork could be called cooperation, and cosmic habitforce could be named nature or habit. Regardless of what the category is called, the essence remains the same. Section number 11 is dedicated to the most often requested reprints of Dr. Hill's "poetic" essays. In this section you will read Dr. Hill's memorable selections that have withstood the test of time.

In reading this anthology, you may consider doing the following things:

1. When you encounter a poem that is or becomes a special favorite, consider memorizing a line or two for positive feedback when you are in a tough situation.

2. Memorize an entire poem until you can recite it at will. Recite it for the fun of it. Not only is this a good mem-

ory technique, but also it serves to underscore the poem's message in your subconscious mind.

3. Journal favorite lines in a notebook and add personal commentary so that you are able to recall why this poem is a favorite.

4. List the poems that inspire you the most. Read them daily or weekly for inspiration.

5. Listen for references to these poems in daily conversion, on television or on the radio. Notice references in printed texts as well.

6. Document which poems move you to action. Why? Keep a list handy and read these poems when you find yourself procrastinating.

7. Write your own inspirational poem based on the theme or structure of one from this anthology.

8. Begin collecting a success anthology of your own. Add poems, short sayings, and quotations that you find appealing and inspirational.

9. Type a favorite piece, print it, frame it, and place it nearby your workspace as a constant reminder of your purpose. Change it weekly.

10. Mentor a friend or family member in the study of inspirational poetry by sharing your favorites at an appropriate time. Or, better yet, buy a second copy of this book and dedicate it to their success on the dedication page.

11. Finally, at the bottom of each poem there is a saying by Napoleon Hill. Reflect on the saying and consider what the quotation has to do with the poem. Afterwards, you may want to author a one sentence explanation of the poem's meaning as it applies to you.

As you begin to chart your course toward success, let these poems and sayings serve as your guideposts. These mile markers, when heeded, tell you that you are on the right path. May you always reach your destination ahead of schedule. As the traditional Irish Blessing states:

> May the road rise up to meet you,
> May the wind always be at your back,
> May the sun shine warm upon your face,
> and rains fall soft upon your fields.
> And until we meet again,
> May God hold you in the palm of His hand.

—Judith Williamson

1

Poems of Purpose

Poems about one's purpose in life can reveal much in a few short lines or stanzas. Difficult thoughts and feelings can be put into words and cause the reader to see a subject from many different perspectives. You may notice that some of the poems in this section are positive and some are negative. Don't let that confuse you. Life is known to have its ups and downs, and good poems show you the many faceted aspects of life. Poetry mirrors life and causes us to reflect on our own choices. If you are looking for achievement and success in your life, remember Dr. Hill's statement: "Definiteness of Purpose is the starting point of all achievement." Everything begins with definiteness of purpose. How is yours?

—Judith Williamson

From the Writings of Dr. Napoleon Hill:

Definiteness of purpose is the starting point of all successful achievement, and it is available to everyone without money and without price except the personal initiative with which to embrace it and use it. Unless you know what you want from life and are determined to get it, you will be forced to accept from life the mere crumbs left by the more fortunate who knew where they were going and had a plan for getting there.

Your major responsibility right now is to find out what you desire in life, where you are going, and what you will do when you get there. This is one responsibility which no one but you can assume. But if you want to rise above mediocrity, you must remember that success begins through Definiteness of Purpose!

Four important things to keep in mind when setting a goal:

1. *Write down your goal.* You will crystallize your thinking. The very act of thinking as you write will create an indelible impression in your memory.

2. *Give yourself a deadline.* Specify a time for achieving your objective. This is important in motivating you: to set out in the direction of your goal and keep moving towards it.

3. *Set your standards high.* Now there seems to be a direct relationship between ease in achieving a goal and the strength of your motives.

   And the higher you set your major goal, generally speaking, the more concentrated will be the effort you make to achieve it.

   The reason—logic will make it mandatory that you at least aim at an intermediate objective as well as an immediate one. So aim higher. And then have immediate and intermediate steps leading towards its achievement.

   This may stimulate your thinking! Where will you be and what will you be doing ten years from today if you keep doing what you are doing now?

4. *Aim high.* It is a peculiar thing that no more effort is required to aim high in life, to demand prosperity and abundance, than is required to accept misery and poverty.

You have to be bold enough to ask of life more than you may, right now, feel you are worth because it is an observable fact that people tend to rise to meet demands that are put upon them.

While it is exceedingly desirable that you blueprint your program from beginning to end, this is not always feasible. One doesn't always know all the answers between the beginning of a great enterprise or journey and its ending. But if you know where you are and where you want to be and you start from where you are to get to where you want to be, you will, if you keep properly motivated, move forward step by step until you get there.

How do you define success? This poem might give you a head start on what to consider when writing your own definition.

Success

It's doing your job the best you can,
And being just to your fellow man.
It's figuring how, and learning why
And looking forward and thinking high.
And dreaming little and doing much:
It's keeping always in closest touch
With what is finest in word and deed:
It's being clean, and it's playing fair:
It's laughing lightly at dame despair;
It's sharing sorrow, and work, and mirth.
And making better this good old earth:
It's serving and striving through strain and stress
It's doing your noblest—that's success.

–ANONYMOUS

Don't be afraid to aim high in choosing my life's goal,
for no matter how high your aim, your
achievements may fall below it.

–NAPOLEON HILL

Begin where you are with what you have.

De Sunflower Ain't De Daisy

De sunflower ain't de daisy, and de melon ain't de rose;
Why is dey all so crazy to be sumfin else dat grows?
Jess stick to de place yo're planted, and do de bes you knows;
Be de sunflower or de daisy, de melon or de rose.
Don't be what you ain't, jess you be what you is,
If yo am not what yo are den you is not what you is,
If yo're jess a little tadpole, don't try to be de frog;
If yo are de tail, don't you try to wag de dawg.
Pass de plate if you can't exhawt and preach;
If yo're jess a little pebble, don't yo try to be de beach;
When a man is what he isn't, den he isn't what he is,
An' as sure as I'm talking, he's a-gwine to get his.

                                        —ANONYMOUS

You may learn many useful facts by studying the honey
bee provided you don't try to show it how to do its job.

                            —NAPOLEON HILL

We must cultivate our dreams and not let them wither and die. Unlike weeds, dreams need ample time to grow and mature before they blossom into success.

Hold Fast Your Dreams

Hold fast your dreams!
Within your heart
Keep one still, secret spot
Where dreams may go,
And, sheltered so,
May thrive and grow
Where doubt and fear are not.
O keep a place apart,
Within your heart,
For little dreams to go!

Think still of lovely things that are not true.
Let wish and magic work at will in you.
Be sometimes blind to sorrow. Make believe!
Forget the calm that lies
In disillusioned eyes.
Though we all know that we must die,
Yet you and I
May walk like gods and be
Even now at home in immortality.

We see so many ugly things—
Deceits and wrongs and quarrelings;
We know, alas! we know

How quickly fade
The color in the west,
The bloom upon the flower,
The bloom upon the breast
And youth's blind hour.
Yet keep within your heart
A place apart
Where little dreams may go,
May thrive and grow.
Hold fast—hold fast your dreams!

–LOUISE DRISCOLL

Always speak when you can say something
encouraging to another.

–NAPOLEON HILL

Be yourself! That is the best gift that you can give to mankind.

Self-Dependence

Weary of myself, and sick of asking
What I am, and what I ought to be,
At this vessel's prow I stand, which bears me
Forwards, forwards, o'er the starlit sea.

And a look of passionate desire
O'er the sea and to the stars I send:
"Ye who from my childhood up have calmed me,
Calm me, ah, compose me to the end!

"Ah, once more," I cried, "ye stars, ye waters,
On my heart your mighty charm renew;
Still, still let me, as I gaze upon you,
Feel my soul becoming vast like you!"

From the intense, clear, star-sown vault of heaven,
Over the lit sea's unquiet way,
In the rustling night-air came the answer:
"Wouldst thou BE as these are? LIVE as they.

"Unaffrighted by the silence round them,
Undistracted by the sights they see,
These demand not that the things without them
Yield them love, amusement, sympathy.

"And with joy the stars perform their shining,
And the sea its long, moon-silver'd roll;
For self-poised they live, nor pine with noting
All the fever of some differing soul.

"Bounded by themselves, and unregardful
In what state God's other works may be,
In their own tasks all their powers pouring,
These attain the mighty life you see."

O air-born voice! long since, severely clear,
A cry like thine in mine own heart I hear:
"Resolve to be thyself; and know that he
Who finds himself, loses his misery!"

—MATTHEW ARNOLD

All riches consist in the habit of clear thinking.

—NAPOLEON HILL

When you find your higher self, you will meet the person you were meant to be.

The One

I knew his face the moment that he passed
 Triumphant in the thoughtless, cruel throng,--
Triumphant, though the quiet, tired eyes
 Showed that his soul had suffered overlong.
And though across his brow faint lines of care
Were etched, somewhat of Youth still lingered there.
I gently touched his arm—he smiled at me—
He was the Man that Once I Meant to Be!

Where I had failed, he'd won from life, Success;
 Where I had stumbled, with sure feet he stood;
Alike—yet unalike—we faced the world,
 And through the stress he found that life was good.
And I? The bitter wormwood in the glass,
The shadowed way along which failures pass!
Yet as I saw him thus, joy came to me—
He was the Man the Once I Meant to Be!

I knew him! And I knew he knew me for
 The man HE might have been. Then did his soul
Thank silently the gods that gave him strength
 To win, while I so sorely missed the goal?
He turned, and quickly in his own firm hand
He took my own—the gulf of Failure spanned, . . .

And that was all—strong, self-reliant, free,
He was the Man that Once I Meant to Be!

We did not speak. But in his sapient eyes
    I saw the spirit that had urged him on,
The courage that had held him through the fight
    Had once been mine, I thought, "Can it be gone?"
He felt that unasked question—felt it so
His pale lips formed the one-word answer, "No!"
-       -   -   -   -   -   -   -   -

Too late to win? No! Not too late for me—
He is the Man that Still I mean to Be!

—EVERARD JACK APPLETON

You can always become the man
you would have liked to be.

—NAPOLEON HILL

Life holds many opportunities for those who approach it with a Positive Mental Attitude.

Opportunity

With doubt and dismay you are smitten
   You think there's no chance for you, son?
Why, the best books haven't been written
   The best race hasn't been run,
The best score hasn't been made yet,
   The best song hasn't been sung,
The best tune hasn't been played yet,
   Cheer up, for the world is young!

No chance? Why the world is just eager
   For things that you ought to create
Its store of true wealth is still meager
   Its needs are incessant and great,
It yearns for more power and beauty
   More laughter and love and romance,
More loyalty, labor and duty,
   No chance—why there's nothing but chance!

For the best verse hasn't been rhymed yet,
   The best house hasn't been planned,
The highest peak hasn't been climbed yet,
   The mightiest rivers aren't spanned,

Don't worry and fret, faint hearted,
    The chances have just begun,
For the Best jobs haven't been started,
    The Best work hasn't been done.

—BERTON BRALEY

Don't be satisfied with being good at your job.
Be the best and you'll soon be indispensable.

–NAPOLEON HILL

Don't miss the boat!

Opportunity

There is a tide in the affairs of men,
Which, taken at the flood, leads on to fortune;
Omitted, all the voyage of their life
Is bound in shallows and in miseries.
On such a full sea are we now afloat;
And we must take the current when it serves,
Or lose our ventures.

—WILLIAM SHAKESPEARE

Burn your bridges behind you, set your mind
on a definite goal and observe how quickly
the world stands aside to let you pass.

–NAPOLEON HILL

Be the one who gets the job done and see how fast the universe arrives on your doorstep.

The Welcome Man

There's a man in the world who is never turned down, wherever he chances to stray; he gets the glad hand in the populous town, or out where the farmers make hay; he's greeted with pleasure on deserts of sand, and deep in the aisles of the woods; wherever he goes there's the welcoming hand—he's The Man Who Delivers the Goods. The failures of life sit around and complain; the gods haven't treated them white; they've lost their umbrellas whenever there's rain, and they haven't their lanterns at night; men tire of the failures who fill with their sighs the air of their own neighborhoods; there's one who is greeted with love-lighted eyes—he's The Man Who Delivers the Goods. One fellow is lazy, and watches the clock, and waits for the whistle to blow; and one has a hammer, with which he will knock, and one tells a story of woe; and one, if requested to travel a mile, will measure the perches and roods; but one does his stunt with a whistle or smile—he's The Man Who Delivers the Goods. One man is afraid that he'll labor too hard—the world isn't yearning for such; and one man is always alert, on his guard, lest he put in a minute too much; and one has a grouch or a temper that's bad, and one is a creature of moods; so it's hey for the joyous and rollicking lad—for the One Who Delivers the Goods!

—WALT MASON

A man's efficiency may be accurately judged by
the amount of supervision he requires.

–NAPOLEON HILL

Even when the going gets tough, I still am in ultimate control of my attitude.

Invictus

Out of the night that covers me
    Back as the Pit from pole to pole,
I thank whatever gods may be
    For my unconquerable soul.

In the fell clutch of circumstance
    I have not winced not cried aloud.
Under the bludgeonings of chance
    My head is bloody, but unbowed.

Beyond this place of wrath and tears
    Looms but the horror of the shade,
And yet the menace of the years
    Finds, and shall find me, unafraid.

It matter not how strait the gate,
    How charged with punishments the scroll,
I am the master of my fate;
    I am the captain of my soul.

—WILLIAM ERNEST HENLEY

The person who controls his mental attitude
may control his destiny.

–NAPOLEON HILL

The road to success is seldom strewn with roses. Rather, it is often muddy and full of potholes. Learn to go the distance.

Challenge

Life, I challenge you to try me,
    Doom me to unending pain;
Stay my hand, becloud my vision,
    Break my heart and then—again.

Shatter every dream I've cherished,
    Fill my heart with ruthless fear;
Follow every smile that cheers me
    With a bitter, blinding tear.

Thus I dare you; you can try me,
    Seek to make me cringe and moan,
Still my unbound soul defies you,
    I'll withstand you—and alone!

—JEAN NETTE

Most men who attain the higher brackets of success
seldom do so until they have undergone some tragedy
which has reached deeply into their souls.

—NAPOLEON HILL

The best command to follow is simply to do good where it is needed.

Not in Vain

If I can stop one heart from breaking,
I shall not live in vain:
If I can ease one life the aching,
Or cool one pain,
Or help one fainting robin
Unto his nest again,
I shall not live in vain.

—EMILY DICKINSON

Happiness may be had only by helping others to find it.
—NAPOLEON HILL

Always keep your eye on the outcome. It will serve as the North Star to guide you home.

Thick Is The Darkness

Thick is the darkness—
   Sunward, O, sunward!
Rough is the highway—
   Onward, still onward!

Dawn harbors surely
   East of the shadows.
Facing us somewhere
   Spread the sweet meadows.

Upward and forward!
   Time will restore us:
Light is above us,
   Rest is before us.

—WILLIAM ERNEST HENLEY

Whatever the mind of man
can conceive and believe,
it can achieve.

—NAPOLEON HILL

In order to straighten out the world, we must first straighten out ourselves.

Good Intentions

The road to hell, they assure me,
With good intentions is paved;
And I know my desires are noble,
But my deeds might brand me depraved.
It's the warped grain in our nature,
And St. Paul has written it true:
"The good that I would I do not;
But the evil I would not I do."

I've met few men who are monsters
When I came to know them inside;
Yet their bearing and dealings external
Are crusted with cruelty, pride,
Scorn, selfishness, envy, indifference,
Greed—why the long list pursue?
The good that they would they do not;
But the evil they would not they do.

Intentions may still leave us beast-like;
With unchangeable purpose we're men.
We must drive the nail home—and then clinch it
Or storms shake it loose again.
In things of great import, in trifles,
We our recreant souls must subdue

Till the evil we would not we do not
And the good that we would we do.

—ST. CLAIR ADAMS

The mistakes others make may provide you
with opportunities for advancement, provided
you are a close observer of little things.

—NAPOLEON HILL

The ladder to success does not begin at the top rung. You must start at the bottom.

Your Mission

If you cannot on the ocean
    Sail among the swiftest fleet,
Rocking on the highest billows,
    Laughing at the storms you meet;
You can stand among the sailors,
    Anchored yet within the bay,
You can lend a hand to help them
    As they launch their boats away.

If you are too weak to journey
    Up the mountain, steep and high,
You can stand within the valley
    While the multitudes go by;
You can chant in happy measure
    As they slowly pass along—
Though they may forget the singer,
    They will not forget the song.

If you cannot in the harvest
    Garner up the richest sheaves,
Many a grain, both ripe and golden,
    Oft the careless reaper leaves;
Go and glean among the briars
    Growing rank against the wall,

For it may be that their shadow
　　Hides the heaviest grain of all.

If you cannot in the conflict
　　Prove yourself a soldier true;
If, where fire and smoke are thickest,
　　There's no work for you to do;
When the battle field is silent,
　　You can go with careful tread;
You can bear away the wounded
　　You can cover up the dead.

Do not then stand idly waiting
　　For some greater work to do;
Fortune is a lazy goddess,
　　She will never come to you;
Go and toil in any vineyard,
　　Do not fear to do and dare.
If you want a field of labor
　　You can find it anywhere.

　　　　　　　　　　　　—ELLEN M. H. GATES

The better portion of a man's pay often consists
in the experience he gets from doing a good job.
　　　　　　　　—NAPOLEON HILL

Always, always, always sail on until your dream is achieved.

Columbus

Behind him lay the gray Azores,
Behind the Gates of Hercules;
Before him not the ghost of shores;
Before him only shoreless seas.
The good mate said: "Now must we pray,
For lo! the very stars are gone.
Brave Adm'r'l, speak; what shall I say?"
"Why, say: 'Sail on! sail on! and on!'"

   "My men grow mutinous day by day;
My men grow ghastly wan and weak."
The stout mate thought of home; a spray
Of salt wave washed his swarthy cheek.
"What shall I say, brave Adm'r'l, say,
If we sight naught but seas at dawn?"
"Why, you shall say at break of day:
'Sail on! sail on! sail on! and on!'"

   They sailed and sailed, as winds might blow,
Until at last the blanched mate said:
"Why, now not even God would know
Should I and all my men fall dead.
These very winds forget their way,
For God from these dread seas is gone.
Now speak, brave Adm'r'l; speak and say----
He said: "Sail on! sail on! and on!"

They sailed. They sailed. Then spake the mate:
"This mad sea shows his teeth to-night.
He curls his lip, he lies in wait,
With lifted teeth, as if to bite!
Brave Adm'r'l, say but one good word:
What shall we do when hope is gone?"
The words leapt like a leaping sword:
"Sail on! sail on! sail on! and on!"

Then, pale and worn, he kept his deck,
And peered through darkness. Ah, that night
Of all dark nights! And then a speck—
A light! A light! A light! A light!
It grew, a starlit flag unfurled!
It grew to be Time's burst of dawn.
He gained a world; he gave that world
Its grandest lesson: "On! sail on!"

–JOAQUIN MILLER

Real courage shows up in a man to best
advantage in the hour of his adversity.
–NAPOLEON HILL

If inspiration does not come to you, go out there are look to the heavens for it!

Per Aspera

Thank God, a man can grow!
   He is not bound
With earthward gaze to creep along the ground:
Though his beginnings be but poor and low,
Thank God, a man can grow!
The fire upon his altars may burn dim,
   The torch he lighted may in darkness fail,
   And nothing to rekindle it avail,--
Yet high beyond his dull horizon's rim,
Arcturus and the Pleiads beckon him.

                      —FLORENCE EARLE COATES

You either ride life or it rides you. Your mental attitude
determines who is rider and who is "horse."
              —NAPOLEON HILL

In defining your major purpose, be certain that it does not harm another human being.

A Little Prayer

That I may not in blindness grope,
　　But that I may with vision clear
Know when to speak a word of hope
　　Or add a little wholesome cheer.

That tempered winds may softly blow
　　Where little children, thinly clad,
Sit dreaming, when the flame is low,
　　Of comforts they never had.

That through the year which lies ahead
　　No heart shall ache, no cheek be wet,
For any word that I have said
　　Or profit I have tried to get.

　　　　　　　　　　　　　　　　　　　－S. E. KISER

To be an educated man I must learn how to get what
I want without violating the rights of others.
－NAPOLEON HILL

Each of us is part of life's continuum and placed here to make a personal contribution.

A Psalm of Life

Tell me not, in mournful numbers,
    Life is but an empty dream!—
For the soul is dead that slumbers,
    And things are not what they seem.

Life is real! Life is earnest!
    And the grave is not its goal;
Dust thou art, to dust returnest,
    Was not spoken of the soul.

Not enjoyment, and not sorrow,
    Is our destined end or way;
But to act, that each to-morrow
    Find us farther than to-day.

Art is long, and Time is fleeting,
    And our hearts, though stout and brave,
Still, like muffled drums, are beating
    Funeral marches to the grave.

In the world's broad field of battle,
    In the bivouac of Life
Be not like dumb, driven cattle!
    Be a hero in the strife!

Trust no Future, howe'er pleasant!
    Let the dead Past bury its dead!
Act ,—act in the living Present!
    Heart within, and God o'erhead!

Lives of great men all remind us
    We can make our lives sublime,
And, departing, leave behind us
    Footprints on the sands of time.

Footprints, that perhaps another,
    Sailing o'er life's solemn main,
A forlorn and shipwrecked brother,
    Seeing, shall take heart again.

Let us, then, be up and doing,
    With a heart for any fate;
Still achieving, still pursuing,
    Learn to labor and to wait.

                    —HENRY WADSWORTH LONGFELLOW

No one can keep me down but myself.
        —NAPOLEON HILL

Be persistent and nothing can defeat you.

Success

If you want a thing bad enough
To go out and fight for it,
Work day and night for it,
Give up your time and your peace and your sleep for it.
If only desire of it
Makes you quite mad enough
Never to tire of it,
Makes you hold all other things tawdry and cheap for it.
If life seems all empty and useless without it
And all that you scheme and you dream is about it,
If gladly you'll sweat for it,
Fret for it,
Plan for it,
Lose all your terror of God or man for it,
If you'll simply go after that thing that you want,
With all your capacity,
Strength and sagacity,
Faith, hope and confidence, stern pertinacity,
If neither cold poverty, famished and gaunt,
Nor sickness not pain
Of body or brain
Can turn you away from the thing that you want,
If dogged and grim you besiege and beset it,
          You'll get it!

                              —BERTON BRALEY

When I have talked myself into what I want,
right there is a place to stop talking and to
begin saying it with deeds.

—NAPOLEON HILL

2

Poems of Faith

Faith must be active, or applied as Dr. Hill tells you, in order to work to your best advantage. To have faith is to have a belief that all will work together for the best possible outcome. Sometimes poems concerning faith seem too magical or too unbelievable to be taken seriously. If you are resistant to the ideas about faith in these poems, consider asking yourself why you feel this way. Do you have an underlying fear or belief that things will turn out badly? Are you hesitant to believe in the possibility of a better than anticipated outcome? As you read these poems on faith, let me suggest that you "suspend your disbelief" momentarily and allow the power of believing to filter into your life. Allowing yourself to experience faith will make a positive difference in your life and in the lives of those you encounter.

—Judith Williamson

From the Writings of Dr. Napoleon Hill:

Fear is faith in reverse gear. Fear is a negative belief in something, and belief is the very foundation of faith.

Faith is a positive mental attitude in action. Your mental attitude is the sum total of your thoughts at any given time.

Faith is a state of mind which has been called "the mainspring of the soul," through which your aims, desires and plans may be translated into their physical equivalents.

Faith is guidance from within which will not bring you that which you seek, but it will show you the path by which you may go after that which you desire.

Characteristics of Faith

1. Faith is a state of mind which enables one to visualize one's central purpose or one's minor plans and purposes as achieved even before beginning the pursuit.

2. Faith is a state of mind which can be induced through intensity of desire backed by persistent suggestion to the subconscious mind that the object of that desire shall become fully realized and attained.

3. Faith begins to take the place of doubt when one recognizes the existence and availability of infinite intelligence.

4. Faith multiplies itself through use! The more one relies upon it, the more pronounced it becomes.

5. Faith is Nature's elixir through the use of which Nature enables man to transmute the impulse of thought into a sky-scraper of riches or a hovel of poverty.

Faith, to work, must be active not passive.

Faith

Faith is not merely praying
　　Upon your knees at night;
Faith is not merely straying
　　Through darkness to the light.

Faith is not merely waiting
　　For glory that may be,
Faith is not merely hating
　　The sinful ecstasy.

Faith is the brave endeavor
　　The splendid enterprise,
The strength to serve, whatever
　　Conditions may arise.

—S. E. KISER

There is no such reality as passive faith.
Action is the first requirement of all faith.
Words, alone, will not serve.
—NAPOLEON HILL

Do not give in to negative thoughts. Be positive about the future.

Be Strong

Be strong!
We are not here to play, to dream, to drift;
We have hard work to do, and loads to lift;
Shun not the struggle—face it; 'tis God's gift.

Be strong!
Say not, "The days are evil. Who's to blame?"
And fold the hands and acquiesce—of shame!
Stand up, speak out, and bravely, in God's name.

Be strong!
It matters not how deep intrenched the wrong,
How hard the battle goes, the day how long;
Faint not—fight on! To-morrow comes the song.

–MALTBIE DAVENPORT BABCOCK

Close the door of fear behind you and see how
quickly the door to faith will open in front of you.

–NAPOLEON HILL

As we learn to take the good with the bad, we will find that there is an ebb and flow to life just as there is with the tides.

Is It Raining, Little Flower?

Is it raining, little flower?
   Be glad of rain.
Too much sun would wither thee,
   'Twill shine again.
The sky is very black, 'tis true,
   But just behind it shines.
      The blue.

Art thou weary, tender heart?
   Be glad of pain;
In sorrow the sweetest thing will grow
   As flowers in the rain.
God watches and thou wilt have sun
   When clouds their perfect work
      Have done.

—ANONYMOUS

The art of being grateful for the blessings you
already possess is of itself the most profound
form of worship, an incomparable gem of prayer.
—NAPOLEON HILL

Perceived difficulties most often are imaginary ones. Take action and watch how soon the walls come tumbling down.

The Bars of Fate

I stood before the bars of Fate
And bowed my head disconsolate;
So high they seemed, so fierce their frown,
I though no hand could break them down.

Beyond them I could hear the songs
Of valiant men who marched in throngs;
And joyful women, fair and free,
Looked back and waved their hands to me.

I did not cry "Too late! too late!"
Or strive to rise, or rail at Fate,
Or pray to God. My coward heart,
Contented, played its foolish part.

So still I sat, the tireless bee
Sped o'er my head, with scorn for me,
And birds who build their nests in air
Beheld me, as I were not there.

From twig to twig, before my face,
The spiders wove their curious lace,
As they a curtain fine would see
Between the hindering bars and me.

Then, sudden change! I head the call
Of wind and wave and waterfall;
From heaven above and earth below
A clear command—"ARISE AND GO!"

I upward sprang in all my strength,
And stretched my eager hands at length
To break the bars—no bars were there;
My fingers fell through empty air!

–ELLEN M. H. GATES

Sound character is man's greatest asset
because it provides the power with which
he may ride the emergencies of life
instead of going down under them.

–NAPOLEON HILL

Look within yourself for your deepest blessings.

The Kingdom of Man

What of the outer drear,
   As long as there's inner light;
As long as the sun of cheer
   Shines ardently bright?

As long as the soul's a-wing,
   As long as the heart is true,
What power hath trouble to bring
   A sorrow to you?

No bar can encage the soul,
   Nor capture the spirit free,
As long as old earth shall roll,
   Or house shall be.

Our world is the world within,
   Our life is the thought we take,
And never an outer sin
   Can mar it or break.

Brood not on the rich man's land,
   Sigh not for miser's gold,
Holding in reach of your hand
   The treasure untold

That lies in the Mines of Heart,
   That rests in the soul alone—
Bid worry and care depart,
   Come into your own!

–JOHN KENDRICK BANGS

If you expect the blessings of prayer, it may help
your cause if you first earn the right to them.

–NAPOLEON HILL

Stay the course. Stay the course. Stay the course.

Resolve

To keep my health!
To do my work!
To live!
To see to it I grow and gain and give!
Never to look behind me for an hour!
To wait in weakness, and to walk in power;
But always fronting onward to the light,
Always and always facing towards the right.
Robbed, starved, defeated, fallen, wide astray—
On, with what strength I have!
Back to the way!

–CHARLOTTE PERKINS GILMAN

The world stands aside and makes room for the person
who knows where he is going and is on the way.

–NAPOLEON HILL

Who do you see when you look in the mirror?

When

When in the silence of the night,
When darkness hugs the world so tight,
When all is hushed and quiet with sleep
Then haunting memories round me creep;
When I can spend that hour alone
And find the man I've never known;
When I can meet him face to face
And there commune with ME apace;

When I can take myself in hand
And measure up just where I stand;
When I can gaze into my heart
And see my worth upon life's chart;
When I can look back o'er the road
And count the times I've shirked my load
And estimate the hours I've spent
On things that were not permanent;

When I can realize the crime
Of spending worthlessly my time;
When I can call things by the name
I ought to, and accept the blame;
When I can place where it belongs
The reason for my countless wrongs;
When I can pile in one great heap
My faults, the harvest I shall reap;

Then knowing what I am can say,
"From this time onward, from today,
I'll work and serve and will to win
To mould a better man within;"
So, when I turn the searchlight on
The faults I had will all be gone,
And there shall stand revealed to me,
The man, God meant that I should be.

–JAMES H. HERON

It will pay anyone to stand on the sideline of life
and watch himself go by now and then, so he
may see himself as the world sees him.

–NAPOLEON HILL

Faith is the opposite of fear.

Grow Old Along With Me!

Grow old along with me!
The best is yet to be,
The last of life, for which the first was made;
Our times are in his hand
Who saith, "A whole I planned,
Youth shows but half; trust God; see all, nor be afraid!"

–ROBERT BROWNING

The odds are a million to one that you have
no worries you couldn't eliminate by merely
changing your mental attitude.

–NAPOLEON HILL

A "no" answer does not mean that it is an inferior one.

Answered Prayer

I asked God for strength,
      that I might achieve;
I was made weak,
      that I might learn to obey.
I asked for health,
      that I might do greater things;
I was given infirmity,
      that I might do better things.
I asked for riches
      that I might be happy;
I was given poverty,
      that I might be wise.
I asked for power,
      that I might have the praise of men;
I was given weakness,
      that I might feel the need of God.
I asked for all things,
      that I might enjoy life;
I was given life,
      that I might enjoy all things.
I received nothing that I asked for—
      but all that I had hoped for;
      almost despite myself,
      my unspoken prayers were answered.
I am, among all men, most richly blessed.

            –UNKNOWN CONFEDERATE SOLDIER

When defeat overtakes you don't put all your
time on counting your losses. Save some of it to
look for your gains and you may find your
gains are greater than your losses.

–NAPOLEON HILL

Today is all you have. Make the most of it.

Look To This Day!

Look to this day!
For it is life, the very life of life.
In its brief course
Lie all the verities and realities of your existence:
> The bliss of growth
> The glory of action
> The splendor of achievement,

For yesterday is but a dream
And tomorrow is only a vision,
But today well lived makes every yesterday a dream of
   happiness
And tomorrow a vision of hope.
Look well, therefore, to this day!
Such is the salutation to the dawn.

–KALIDASA

There's an abundance of everything for
the man who knows what he wants.

–NAPOLEON HILL

3

Poems about Going the Extra Mile

Napoleon Hill has stated that if you only use one success principle after you have discovered your definite major purpose that it should be the principle of Going the Extra Mile. Dr. Hill uses the acronym GEM to describe this principle because he believes that it is a real jewel. When you use this principle unselfishly, the Law of Compensation and the Law of Increasing Returns will reward you over and above your personal contribution.

Begin a trial use of this principle if you doubt its merit. Practice the habit of going the extra mile at least once a day without the expectation of receiving anything back for the services you have rendered. Keep a daily log for a month of what you did above and beyond your normal duties. Afterwards, reflect on the compensation or benefits you have received from this practice. You will be surprised at the rewards that you can soon enumerate.

—Judith Williamson

From the Writings of Dr. Napoleon Hill:

Down through the years I have observed that no one ever reaches a high station in life without following the habit of

Going the Extra Mile. Also, that no one ever follows this habit conscientiously without eventually receiving benefits far out of proportion to the usual commercial value of the services rendered. This habit is the only legitimate reason for asking for a promotion or an increase in pay, and the person who recognizes this truth and applies it places himself in a position to fix his own wages and his choice of positions if he works for wages.

One of the great advantages of the habit of rendering more service and better service than one is paid for is the fact that one does not have to ask permission of anyone else to render this sort of service. Following this habit brings one to the favorable attention of those who can and will properly recognize and reward it, whether that person is in business for himself, or a profession, or works for wages. If one employer fails to do so his competitor will be quick to do so.

Among the many sound reasons for rendering more service and better service than expected are the following:

1. This habit turns the spotlight of favorable attention upon those who develop it.

2. This habit enables one to profit by the law of contrast, since the majority of people have formed and apply the opposing habit, by rendering as little service as they can.

3. This habit gives one the benefit of the law of Increasing Returns and insures one against the disadvantages of the law of Decreasing Returns, thus eventually enabling one to receive more pay than one would receive without this habit.

4. This habit insures one preferred employment at preferred wages and permanency of employment as long as there is employment to be had. The person who practices this habit is the last to be removed from the pay-roll when business is poor and the first to be taken back after a lay-off.

5. This habit develops greater skill, efficiency, and also greater earning ability and tends to give one preference over others.

6. This habit makes one practically indispensable to one's employer because it is a habit not found in the majority of people, and because it induces employers to relegate greater responsibilities to those who practice it. The capacity to assume responsibility is the quality which brings the highest monetary returns.

7. This habit leads to promotion because it indicates that those who practice it have ability for supervision and leadership not found in those who follow the opposite habit.

8. This habit enables one to set one's own salary. If it cannot be obtained from one employer, it may be obtained from his competitor.

Always go the extra mile when creating new and keeping old friendships.

New Friends and Old Friends

Make new friends, but keep the old;
Those are silver, these are gold.
New-made friendships, like new wine,
Age will mellow and refine.
Friendships that have stood the test—
Time and change—are surely best;
Brow may wrinkle, hair grow gray,
Friendship never knows decay.
For 'mid old friends, tried and true,
Once more we our youth renew.
But old friends, alas! may die,
New friends must their place supply.
Cherish friendship in your breast—
New is good, but old is best;
Make new friends, but keep the old;
Those are silver, these are gold.

—JOSEPH PARRY

No man can become a permanent success
without taking others along with him.
—NAPOLEON HILL

The smallest action has the potential for creating much future good.

Wishing

Do you wish the world were better?
    Let me tell you what to do.
Set a watch upon your actions,
    Keep them always straight and true.
Rid your mind of selfish motives,
    Let your thoughts be clean and high.
You can make a little Eden
    Of the sphere you occupy.

Do you wish the world were wiser?
    Well, suppose you make a start,
By accumulating wisdom
    In the scrapbook of your heart;
Do not waste one page on folly;
    Live to learn, and learn to live.
If you want to give men knowledge
    You must get it, ere you give.

Do you wish the world were happy?
    Then remember day by day
Just to scatter seeds of kindness
    As you pass along the way,
For the pleasures of the many
    May be ofttimes traced to one,

As the hand that plants an acorn
  Shelters armies from the sun.

–ELLA WHEELER WILCOX

The one and only thing any man has to give in return
for the material riches he desires is useful service.

–NAPOLEON HILL

Words can hurt or heal. Make your song a blessing not a curse.

The Arrow and The Song

I shot an arrow into the air,
It fell to earth, I knew not where;
For, so swiftly it flew, the sight
Could not follow it in its flight.

I breathed a song into the air,
It fell to earth, I knew not where;
For who has sight so keen and strong,
That it can follow the flight of song?

Long, long afterward, in an oak
I found the arrow, still unbroke;
And the song, from beginning to end,
I found again in the heart of a friend.

                  –HENRY WADSWORTH LONGFELLOW

Every time you influence another person to do a better
job you benefit him and increase your own value.
            –NAPOLEON HILL

Remember the good that you do and celebrate yourself.

Two At a Fireside

I built a chimney for a comrade old,
    I did the service not for hope or hire—
And then I traveled on in winter's cold,
    Yet all the day I glowed before the fire.

–EDWIN MARKHAM

The most profitable time any man spends
is that for which he is not directly paid.

–NAPOLEON HILL

When you express yourself positively, positive things return to you.

A Smiling Paradox

I've squandered smiles to-day,
    And, strange to say,
Altho' my frowns with care I've stowed away,
To-night I'm poorer far in frowns than at the start;
    While in my heart,
Wherein my treasures best I store,
I find my smiles increased by several score.

–JOHN KENDRICK BANGS

A smiling face often defeats the cruelest of
antagonists, for it is hard to argue with the
man who smiles when he speaks.

–NAPOLEON HILL

Let your light shine forth.

Good Deeds

How far that little candle throws his beams!
So shines a good deed in a naughty world.
Heaven doth with us as we with torches do;
Not light them for themselves; for if our virtues
Did not go forth of us, 'twere all alike
As if we had them not.

–WILLIAM SHAKESPEARE

The most successful men are those who
serve the greatest number of people.

–NAPOLEON HILL

Recognize somebody and introduce them to their higher self.

Appreciation

Life's a bully good game with its kicks and cuffs—
  Some smile, some laugh, some bluff;
Some carry a load too heavy to bear
  While some push on with never a care,
But the load will seldom heavy be
  When I appreciate you and you appreciate me.

He who lives by the side of the road
  And helps to bear his brother's load
May seem to travel lone and long
  While the world goes by with a merry song,
But the heart grows warm and sorrows flee
  When I appreciate you and you appreciate me.

When I appreciate you and you appreciate me,
  The road seems short to victory;
It buoys one up and calls "Come on,"
  And days grow brighter with the dawn;
There is no doubt or mystery
  When I appreciate you and you appreciate me.

It's the greatest thought in heaven or earth—
  It helps us know our fellow's worth;
There'd be no wars or bitterness,
  No fear, no hate, no grasping; yes,

It makes work play, and the careworn free
When I appreciate you and you appreciate me.
–WILLIAM JUDSON KIBBY

Friendly counsel carries more weight
than unfriendly criticism.
–NAPOLEON HILL

How do you spend your days? Are you guilty of sins of omission?

You May Count That Day

If you sit down at set of sun
And count the acts that you have done,
    And, counting, find
One self-denying deed, one word
That eased the heart of him who heard—
    One glance most kind,
That fell like sunshine where it went—
Then you may count that day well spent.

But if, through all the livelong day,
You've cheered no heart, by yea or nay—
    If, through it all
You've nothing done that you can trace
That brought the sunshine to one face—
    No act most small
That helped some soul and nothing cost—
Then count that day as worse than lost.

–GEORGE ELIOT

Sooner or later the world will find you out and
reward you or penalize you for exactly what you are.

–NAPOLEON HILL

4

Poems of Personal Initiative

Personal initiate requires us to take action, and we know action is the master key to success. Thought + Action = Success. By being active, an individual can refine his definite major purpose, inspire others to follow him, and allow faith to offer guidance in the form inspiration.

Personal initiative means taking the very next action that can be taken that will lead you toward your goal. It does not mean sitting around for the "right" opportunity to knock on your front door. We really do create our destiny by the thoughts that we think and the actions that we take. Are the actions you took today leading you toward or away from your ultimate goal?

—Judith Williamson

From the Writings of Dr. Napoleon Hill:

Personal initiative bears the same relationship to an individual that a self-starter bears to an automobile. It is the power that starts all action. It is the power that assures completion of anything one begins.

There are many "starters" but few "finishers." Personal initiative is the dynamo that pushes the faculty of the imagination into action. It is the process of translating your definite major purpose into its physical or financial equivalent. It is the quality that creates a major purpose, as well as all the minor purposes.

Memorize, understand, and repeat frequently throughout the day:

> *What the mind can conceive and believe,*
> *the mind can achieve.*

It is a form of self-suggestion. It is a self-motivator to success. When it becomes a part of you, you dare to aim higher.

Always know your true worth and do not be afraid to ask for it.

My Wage

I bargained with Life for a penny,
　　And Life would pay no more,
However I begged at evening
　　When I counted my scanty store;

For Life is a just employer,
　　He gives you what you ask,
But once you have set the wages,
　　Why, you must bear the task.

I worked for a menial's hire,
　　Only to learn, dismayed,
That any wage I had asked of Life,
　　Life would have paid.

—JESSIE B. RITTENHOUSE

This is a fine world for the man who knows precisely
what he wants in life and is busy getting it.

–NAPOLEON HILL

Set your sails for uncharted worlds.

The Things That Haven't Been Done Before

The things that haven't been done before,
    Those are the things to try;
Columbus dreamed of an unknown shore
    At the rim of the far-flung sky,
And his heart was bold and his faith was strong
    As he ventured in dangers new,
And he paid no heed to the jeering throng
    Or the fears of the doubting crew.

The many will follow the beaten track
    With guideposts on the way,
They live and have lived for ages back
    With a chart for every day.
Someone has told them it's safe to go
    On the road he has traveled o'er,
And all that they ever strive to know
    Are the things that were known before.

A few strike out, without map or chart,
    Where never a man has been,
From the beaten paths they draw apart
    To see what no man has seen,
There are deeds they hunger alone to do;
    Though battered and bruised and sore,
They blaze the path for the many, who
    Do nothing not done before.

The things that haven't been done before
　　Are the tasks worth while to-day;
Are you one of the flock that follows, or
　　Are you one that shall lead the way?
Are you one of the timid souls that quail
　　At the jeers of a doubting crew,
Or dare you, whether you win or fail,
　　Strike out for a goal that's new?

–EDGAR A. GUEST

Your ship will not come in
unless you have first sent it out.

–NAPOLEON HILL

Who can measure the value of one action?

Just One

One song can spark a moment,
One flower can wake the dream.
One tree can start a forest,
One bird can herald spring.
One smile begins a friendship,
One handclasp lifts a soul.
One star can guide a ship at sea,
One word can frame the goal
One vote can change a nation,
One sunbeam lights a room
One candle wipes out darkness,
One laugh will conquer gloom.
One step must start each journey.
One word must start each prayer.
One hope will raise our spirits,
One touch can show you care.
One voice can speak with wisdom,
One heart can know what's true,

One life can make a difference,
You see, it's up to you!

                           —AUTHOR UNKNOWN

The little job well done is the first step
toward a bigger one.

–NAPOLEON HILL

The time is never perfect. Begin anyway.

The Winds of Fate

One ship drives east and another drives west
  With the selfsame winds that blow.
    'Tis the set of the sails
    And not the gales
Which tells us the way to go.

Like the winds of the sea are the ways of fate,
  As we voyage along through life:
    'Tis the set of a soul
    That decides its goal,
And not the calm or the strife.

—ELLA WHEELER WILCOX

All enduring success begins with a success
consciousness backed by a definite plan.

—NAPOLEON HILL

Each day you are given a gift of 24 hours. Will you use it, or discard it unopened?

To-Day

So here hath been dawning
   Another blue day;
Think, wilt thou let it
   Slip useless away?

Out of Eternity
   This new day is born;
Into Eternity,
   At night will return.

Behold it aforetime
   No eye ever did;
So soon it for ever
   From all eyes is hid.

Here hath been dawning
   Another blue day;
Think, wilt thou let it
   Slip useless away?

–THOMAS CARLYLE

Life says: "Make good or make room but don't make excuses."
–NAPOLEON HILL

Be not afraid. Be bold. Live every moment of your life.

Cowards

Cowards die many times before their deaths:
The valiant never taste of death but once.
Of all the wonders that I yet have heard,
It seems to me most strange that men should fear;
Seeing that death, a necessary end,
Will come, when it will come.

–WILLIAM SHAKESPEARE

Haven't you noticed that a man can always find
a way to do that which he must do or else?

–NAPOLEON HILL

Go or stop. These are the two choices. One speaks to life, the other to death.

Keep a-Goin'

If you strike a thorn or rose,
    Keep a-goin'!
If it hails or if it snows,
    Keep a-goin'!
'Taint no use to sit an' whine
When the fish ain't on your line;
Bait your hook an' keep a tryin'—
    Keep a-goin'!

When the weather kills your crop,
    Keep a-goin'!
Though 'tis work to reach the top,
    Keep a-goin'!
S'pose you're out o' ev'ry dime,
Gittin' broke ain't any crime;
Tell the world you're feelin' *prime*—
    Keep a-goin'!

When it looks like all is up,
    Keep a-goin'!
See the wild birds on the wing,
Hear the bells that sweetly ring,
When you feel like surgin', sing—
    Keep a-goin'!

—FRANK L. STANTON

A positive mental attitude is an irresistible force
that knows no such thing as an immovable body.

–NAPOLEON HILL

Everyone admires the "comeback kid." Come back to your higher self.

The Has-Beens

I read the papers every day, and oft encounter tales which show there's hope for every jay who in life's battle fails. I've just been reading of a gent who joined the has-been ranks, at fifty years without a cent, or credit at the banks. But undismayed he buckled down, refusing to be beat, and captured fortune and renown; he's now on Easy Street. Men say that fellows down and out ne'er leave the rocky track, but facts will show, beyond a doubt, that has-beens do come back. I know, for I who write this rhyme, when forty-odd years old, was down and out, without a dime, my whiskers full of mold. By black disaster I was trounced until it jarred my spine; I was a failure so pronounced I didn't need a sign. And after I had soaked my coat, I said (at forty-three), "I'll see if I can catch the goat that has escaped from me." I labored hard; I strained my dome, to do my daily grind, until in triumph I came home, my billy-goat behind. And any man who still has health may with the winners stack, and have a chance at fame and wealth—for has-beens do come back.

–WALT MASON

The man who complains he never had a chance
probably hasn't the courage to take a chance.
–NAPOLEON HILL

Are you stopping just short of success?

Have You Thought?

Have you thought, when feeling weary
    With the trials of the day,
Of the thousand wasted chances
    Which the hours have borne away?

Have you thought about the blessings
    That surround you all the time,
And that grumbling in their presence
    Is a weakness, nay, a crime?

Have you thought of all you're missing
    While you waste time and complain,
And what fortune may await you,
    If you only try again?

—ANONYMOUS

A man is never a failure until he accepts
defeat as permanent and quits trying.

—NAPOLEON HILL

The mind is a garden. Plant good thoughts and reap a bountiful harvest.

The Garden of Life

First, Plant Five Rows of P's
 Presence
 Promptness
 Preparation
 Perseverance
 Purity

Next, Plant Three Rows of Squash
 Squash gossip
 Squash indifference
 Squash unjust criticism

Then Plant Five Rows of Lettuce
 Let us be faithful to duty
 Let us be unselfish and loyal
 Let us obey the rules and regulations
 Let us be true to our obligations and
 Let us love one another

No Garden is Complete Without Turnips
 Turn up for meetings
 Turn up with a smile
 Turn up with new ideas
 Turn up with determination to make everything
  count for something
 Good and worthwhile.

       –ANONYMOUS

Nature yields her most profound secrets to
the man who is determined to uncover them.
—NAPOLEON HILL

5

Poems of Positive Mental Attitude

Positive Mental Attitude is the right mental attitude in all circumstances. It puts the spring in our step, the light in our eyes, the smile in our voice, and the laughter in our hearts. When we remain positive, we have an optimistic outlook on life. Life is fun, friends are a blessing, goodness abounds, and lightness prevails. Unfortunately, we are not born with or without a positive outlook on life. We cultivate it ourselves based on our experiences and our assessment of these experiences. Bad things do happen to undeserving people, however, it is the viewpoint we take on the event and not the actual event that shapes our attitude. No matter what happened to Napoleon Hill's partner, W. Clement Stone, he always responded with a resounding "That's good!" Through this method he conditioned his mind to focus only on the positive side of life. Mr. Stone was a master at this technique and you can be too. Make "That's good!" a mantra that you use many times each day.

—Judith Williamson

From the Writings of Dr. Napoleon Hill:

Mental attitude is a two-way gate across the path of life which can be swung one way into the path that leads to success and the other way into the road to failure. What a profound thought it is to recognize that the one thing which can bring us success or failure, bless us with peace of mind or curse us with misery all the days of our lives, is simply the privilege of taking possession of our own minds and guiding them to whatever ends we choose, through our mental attitude.

The starting point of control of the mental attitude is motive and desire. No one ever does anything without a motive or motives for doing it, and the stronger the motive the easier it is to control and condition the mental attitude.

You have within you a sleeping giant who is ready to be awakened and directed by you to the performance of any sort of service you desire. And when you wake up some morning and find yourself on the success beam and in the upper brackets of success you will wonder why you had not sooner discovered that you had all of the makings of a big success.

Let these single ingredient self-motivators give you instant nourishment!

God is always a good God!

Day by day, in every way, through the grace of God, you are getting better and better!

Have the courage to face the truth!

What the mind can conceive and believe, the mind can achieve!

Every adversity has the seed of a greater benefit!

You can do it if you believe you can!

Thinking makes it so. So, THINK.

Thinking

"If you think you are beaten, you are,
  If you think you dare not, you don't.
If you like to win, but you think you can't,
  It is almost certain you won't.

"If you think you'll lose, you're lost,
  For out in the world we find,
Success begins with a fellow's will—
  It's all in the state of mind.

"If you think your are outclassed, you are,
  You've got to think high to rise,
You've got to be sure of yourself before
  You can ever win a prize.

"Life's battles don't always go
  To the stronger or faster man,
But soon or late the man who wins
  Is the man WHO THINKS HE CAN!"

—W. D. WINTLE

It isn't defeat, but it's your mental attitude
toward it that whips you.
—NAPOLEON HILL

Our perception of things makes them either good or bad.

This World

This world that we're a-livin' in
  Is mighty hard to beat;
You git a thorn with every rose,
  But ain't the roses sweet!

—FRANK L. STANTON

Remember that every defeat and every
disappointment and every adversity carries
the seed of an equivalent benefit.

—NAPOLEON HILL

Take the best, and leave the rest.

Age is a Quality of Mind

Age is a quality of mind.
If you have left your dreams behind,
If hope is cold,
If you no longer look ahead,
If your ambitions' fires are dead—
Then you are old.

But if from life you take the best,
And if in life you keep the jest,
If love you hold;
No matter how the years go by,
No matter how the birthdays fly—
You are not old.

—ANONYMOUS

Your true age is determined by your mental attitude,
not by the years that you have lived.
—NAPOLEON HILL

Enhance the positive. Look to the best.

Gray Days

Hang the gray days!
The deuce-to-pay days!
The feeling-blue and nothing-to-do days!
The sit-by-yourself-for-there's-nothing-new days!
When the cat that Care killed without excuse
With your inner self's crying, "Oh, what's the use?"
And you wonder whatever is going to become of you,
And you feel that a cipher expresses the sum of you;
And you know that you'll never,
Oh, never, be clever,
Spite of all your endeavor
Or hard work or whatever!
Oh, gee!
What a mix-up you see
When you look at the world where you happen to be!
Where strangers are hateful and friends are a bore,
And you know in your heart you will smile nevermore!
Gee, kid!
Clap on the lid!
It is all a mistake! Give your worries the skid!
There are sunny days coming
    Succeeding the blue
And bees will be humming
    Making honey for you,
And your heart will be singing
    The merriest tune

While April is bringing
  A May and a June!
Gray days? Play days!
Joy-bringing pay days
And heart-lifting May days!
The sun will be shining in just a wee while
So smile!

–GRIFFITH ALEXANDER

When enthusiasm is a habit fear and
worry do not hang around.

–NAPOLEON HILL

Find a need and fill it.

One of These Days

Say! Let's forget it! Let's put it aside!
Life is so large and the world is so wide.
Days are so short and there's so much to do,
What if it was false—there's plenty that's true.
Say! Let's forget it! Let's brush it away
Now and forever, so what do you say?
All of the bitter words said may be praise
One of these days.

Say! Let's forget it! Let's wipe off the slate,
Find something better to cherish than hate.
There's so much good in the world that we've had,
Let's strike a balance and cross off the bad.
Say! Let's forgive it, whatever it be,
Let's not be slaves when we ought to be free.
We shall be walking in sunshiny ways
One of these days.

Say! Let's not mind it! Let's smile it away,
Bring not a withered rose from yesterday;
Flowers are so fresh from the wayside and wood,
Sorrows are blessings but half understood.
Say! Let's not mind it, however it seems,
Hope is so sweet and holds so many dreams;
All of the sere fields with blossoms shall blaze
One of these days.

Say! Let's not take it so sorely to heart!
Hates may be friendships just drifted apart,
Failure be genius not quite understood,
We could all help folks so much if we would.
Say! Let's get closer to somebody's side,
See what his dreams are and learn how he tried,
See if our scoldings won't give way to praise
One of these days.

Say! Let's not wither! Let's branch out and rise
Out of the byways and nearer the skies.
Let's spread some shade that's refreshing and deep
Where some tired traveler may lie down and sleep.
Say! Let's not tarry! Let's do it right now;
So much to do if we just find out how!
We may not be here to help folks or praise
One of these days.

–JAMES W. FOLEY

Men who get ahead successfully have
no time to waste on fault-finding.

–NAPOLEON HILL

Begin each of your days with this "to do" list.

On This Day

On This Day—
Mend a quarrel,
Search out a forgotten friend,
Dismiss a suspicion and replace it with trust,
Write a letter to someone who misses you,
Encourage a youth who has lost faith,
Keep a promise,
Forget an old grudge,
Examine your demands on others and vow to reduce them,
Fight for a principle,
Express your gratitude,
Overcome an old fear,
Take two minutes to appreciate the beauty of nature,
Tell someone you love him.
Tell him again,
And again,
And again.

—ANONYMOUS

A positive mind finds a way it can be done, a negative
mind looks for all the ways it can't be done.
—NAPOLEON HILL

Define yourself first and then measure your success by your own yardstick.

My Creed

To live as gently as I can;
To be, no matter where, a man;
To take what comes of good or ill
And cling to faith and honor still;
To do my best, and let that stand
The record of my brain and hand;
And then, should failure come to me,
Still work and hope for victory.

To have no secret place wherein
I stoop unseen to shame or sin;
To be the same when I'm alone
As when my every deed is known;
To live undaunted, unafraid
Of any step that I have made;
To be without pretense or sham
Exactly what men think I am.

To leave some simple mark behind
To keep my having lived in mind;
If enmity to aught I show,
To be an honest, generous foe,
To play my little part, not whine

That greater honors are not mine.
This, I believe, is all I need
For my philosophy and creed.

—EDGAR A. GUEST

A man who is at peace with himself
is also at peace with the world.

—NAPOLEON HILL

Sure cures for depression and boredom are work.

WORK

"A Song of Triumph"

WORK!
Thank God for the might of it,
The ardor, the urge, the delight of it—
Work that springs from the heart's desire,
Setting the brain and the soul on fire—
Oh, what is so good as the heat of it,
And what is so glad as the beat of it,
And what is so kind as the stern command,
Challenging brain and heart and hand?

Work!
Thank God for the pride of it,
For the beautiful, conquering tide of it,
Sweeping the life in its furious flood,
Thrilling the arteries, cleansing the blood,
Mastering stupor and dull despair,
Moving the dreamer to do and dare.
Oh, what is so good as the urge of it,
And what is so glad as the surge of it,
And what is so strong as the summons deep,
Rousing the torpid soul from sleep?

Work!
Thank God for the pace of it,

For the terrible, keen, swift race of it;
Fiery steeds in full control,
Nostrils a-quiver to greet the goal.
Work, the Power that drives behind,
Guiding the purposes, taming the mind,
Holding the runaway wishes back,
Reining the will to one steady track,
Speeding the energies faster, faster,
Triumphing over disaster.
Oh, what is so good as the pain of it,
And what is so great as the gain of it?
And what is so kind as the cruel goad,
Forcing us on through the rugged road?

Work!
Thank God for the swing of it,
For the clamoring, hammering ring of it,
Passion and labor daily hurled
On the mighty anvils of the world.
Oh, what is so fierce as the flame of it?
And what is so huge as the aim of it?
Thundering on through dearth and doubt,
Calling the plan of the Maker out.
Work, the Titan; Work, the friend,
Shaping the earth to a glorious end,
Draining the swamps and blasting the hills,
Doing whatever the Spirit wills—
Rending a continent apart,
To answer the dream of the Master heart.
Thank God for a world where none may shirk—
Thank God for the splendor of work!

                                    —ANGELA MORGAN

The happiest men are those who have learned
to mix play with their work and bind the
two together with enthusiasm.

–NAPOLEON HILL

Do you live in your soul's attic or basement?

The Inner Light

He that has light within his own breast
May sit i' the center, and enjoy bright day:
But he that hides a dark soul and foul thoughts
Benighted walks under the midday sun;
Himself is his own dungeon.

–JOHN MILTON

Every thought a man releases becomes a
permanent part of his character.

–NAPOLEON HILL

A successful man never stoops to mistreating his subordinates.

Man's Measurement

A man's no bigger than the way
   He treats his fellow man!
This standard has his measure been
   Since time itself began!
He's measured not by titles or creed
   High-sounding though they be;
Nor by the gold that's put aside;
   Nor by his sanctity!
He's measured not by social rank,
   When character's the test;
Nor by his earthly pomp or show,
   Displaying wealth possessed!
He's measured by his justice right,
   His fairness at his play.
His squareness in all his dealings made,
   His honest, upright way.
These are his measures, ever near
   To serve him when they can;
For man's no bigger than the way
   He treats his fellow man.

—ANONYMOUS

You may usually judge the nature of a man's character by
the scope of his courtesy to his subordinates.
—NAPOLEON HILL

Keep close watch on who you associate with because, like it or not, we are judged by the friends we keep.

You Tell on Yourself

You tell on yourself by the friends you seek
By the very manner in which you speak
By the way you enjoy your leisure time,
And the use you make of dollar and dime.

You tell who you are by the way you walk
The things in which you delight to talk.
The kind of things that make your laugh
The records you play on the phonograph.

You tell on yourself by the clothes you wear
The spirit in which your burdens bear
The manner in which you bear defeat
And so simple a thing as what you eat.

By the book you choose from the well-filled shelf
In this way you more or less tell on yourself.
So it really doesn't make a particle of sense
To try and keep up a false pretense.

—ANONYMOUS

Sometimes when a man really finds himself, he isn't proud of the companions he finds himself with.

–NAPOLEON HILL

Praise instead of complain.

The Pessimist

Nothing to do but work,
　　Nothing to eat but food,
Nothing to wear but clothes
　　To keep one from going nude.

Nothing to breathe but air
　　Quick as a flash 'tis gone;
Nowhere to fall but off,
　　Nowhere to stand but on.

Nothing to comb but hair,
　　Nowhere to sleep but in bed,
Nothing to weep but tears,
　　Nothing to bury but dead.

Nothing to sing but songs,
　　Ah, well, alas! alack!
Nowhere to go but out,
　　Nowhere to come but back.

Nothing to see but sights,
　　Nothing to quench but thirst,
Nothing to have but what we've got;
　　Thus thro' life we are cursed.

Nothing to strike but a gait;
   Everything moves that goes.
Nothing at all but common sense
   Can ever withstand these woes.

—BEN KING

A man's likes and dislikes come back to him from
unexpected sources and often greatly multiplied.

—NAPOLEON HILL

Be determined to remain positive.

Keep on Keepin' On

If the day looks kinder gloomy
And your chances kinder slim,
If the situation's puzzlin'
And the prospect's awful grim,
If perplexities keep pressin'
Till hope is nearly gone,
Just bristle up and grit your teeth
And keep on keepin' on.

Frettin' never wins a fight
And fumin' never pays;
There ain't no use in broodin'
In these pessimistic ways;
Smile just kinder cheerfully
Though hope is nearly gone,
And bristle up and grit your teeth
And keep on keepin' on.

There ain't no use in growlin'
And grumblin' all the time,
When music's ringin' everywhere
And everything's a rhyme.
Just keep on smilin' cheerfully
If hope is nearly gone,
And bristle up and grit your teeth
And keep on keepin' on.

                              —ANONYMOUS

When you close the door of your mind to negative thoughts, the door of opportunity opens to you.

–NAPOLEON HILL

Laughter draws people closer to you, but crying repels them.

Solitude

Laugh, and the world laughs with you;
    Weep, and you weep alone.
For the sad old earth must borrow its mirth,
    But has trouble enough of its own.
Sing, and the hills will answer;
    Sigh, it is lost on the air.
The echoes bound to a joyful sound,
    But shrink from voicing care.

Rejoice, and men will seek you;
    Grieve, and they turn and go.
They want full measure of all your pleasure,
    But they do not need your woe.
Be glad, and your friends are many;
    Be sad, and you lose them all.
There are none to decline your nectared wine,
    But alone you must drink life's gall.

Feast, and your halls are crowded;
    Fast, and the world goes by.
Succeed and give, and it helps you live,
    But no man can help you die.
There is room in the halls of pleasure
    For a long and lordly train,
But one by one we must all file on
    Through the narrow aisles of pain.

                –ELLA WHEELER WILCOX

When the going is hardest, just put on a smile and you'll get there sooner than some who find the going easy.

−NAPOLEON HILL

Character is built slowly brick by brick over the years, but can be dismantled by the wrecking ball of a bad reputation in less than a minute.

A Good Name

Good name in man and woman, dear my lord,
Is the immediate jewel of their souls:
Who steals my purse steals trash; 'tis something, nothing;
'Twas mine, 'tis his, and has been slave to thousands;
But he that filches from me my good name
Robs me of that which not enriches him,
And makes me poor indeed.

–WILLIAM SHAKESPEARE

Attend well to your character and your
reputation will look out for itself.

–NAPOLEON HILL

Look your Pilot in the eye and tell him that you stood your watch well when it is time to report.

Crossing the Bar

Sunset and evening star,
  And one clear call for me!
And may there be no moaning of the bar,
  When I put out to sea.

But such a tide as moving seems asleep,
  Too full for sound and foam,
When that which drew from out the boundless deep
  Turns again home.

Twilight and evening bell,
  And after that the dark!
Any may there be no sadness of farewell,
  When I embark;

For though from out our bourne of Time and Place
  The flood may bear me far,
I hope to see my Pilot face to face
  When I have crossed the bar.

       –ALFRED TENNYSON

The greatest of all thrills is that which comes from recognition that one is the complete master of himself.
    –NAPOLEON HILL

Be careful that you do not confuse intentions with actions. They are not the same nor equal.

God

I think about God.
    Yet I talk of small matters.
Now isn't it odd
    How my idle tongue chatters!
Of quarrelsome neighbors,
    Fine weather and rain,
Indifferent labors,
    Indifferent pain,
Some trivial style
    Fashion shifts with a nod.
And yet all the while
    I am thinking of God.

—GAMALIEL BRADFORD

All you are or ever shall become is the result
of the use to which you put your mind.
—NAPOLEON HILL

6

Poems of Self-Discipline

Self-discipline means taking control of your own mind—your time and talents—and using all the tools in your toolkit to further yourself toward your ultimate goal. This is not an easy principle to employ since it involves making "good for you choices." Many times, we would rather travel down easy street and forego the potholes and hurdles that life places in the way of those who practice self-discipline. Just remember that no one said the race was going to be easy, it is only said that at the finish line the race is worthwhile.

Practice self-discipline and run the race like a thoroughbred. Give what it takes, and then demand the trophy.

—Judith Williamson

From the Writings of Dr. Napoleon Hill:

Self-discipline is the principle by which one may voluntarily shape the patterns of thought to harmonize with his aims and purposes.

This privilege carries with it a heavy responsibility because it is the one privilege which determines, more than all the others, the position in life which each man shall occupy.

You can keep your mind trained on that which you desire from life and get just that! Or you can feed it on thoughts of that which you do not desire and it will, as unerringly, bring you just that. Your thought habits evolve from the food that your mind dwells upon.

Here's how to use your knowledge regarding self-discipline:

1. Concentrate on one principle for an entire week, every day of the week. Respond by proper action every time an occasion arises.

2. And then, start the second week on the second principle or virtue. Let the first be taken over by your subconscious mind. Should an occasion arise when the employment of a previous principle flashes into your conscious mind, use the self-starter DO IT NOW! and then ACT! Continue to concentrate on one principle at a time each week and leave the others to be executed by the habits established in your subconscious as the occasion arises.

3. When the series is completed, start over again. Thus at the end of a year, you will have completed the entire cycle four times.

4. When you have acquired a desired characteristic, substitute a new principle for a new virtue, attitude, or activity that you may wish to develop.

It's either *can* or *can't*. You decide.

Always Finish

If a task is once begun
Never leave it till it's done.
Be the labor great or small,
Do it well or not at all.

—UNKNOWN

When a man gets to where he can manage himself,
he is ready to start managing others.

—NAPOLEON HILL

You've heard it before, and it's always a good message. Finish what you start.

Can't

Can't is the worst word that's written or spoken;
   Doing more harm here than slander and lies;
On it is many a strong spirit broken,
   And with it many a good purpose dies.
It springs from the lips of the thoughtless each morning
   And robs us of courage we need through the day:
It rings in our ears like a timely-sent warning
   And laughs when we falter and fall by the way.

Can't is the father of feeble endeavor,
   The parent of terror and half-hearted work;
It weakens the efforts of artisans clever,
   And makes of the toiler an indolent shirk.
It poisons the soul of the man with a vision,
   It stifles in infancy many a plan;
It greets honest toiling with open derision
   And mocks at the hopes and the dreams of a man.

Can't is a word none should speak without blushing;
   To utter it should be a symbol of shame;
Ambition and courage it daily is crushing;
   It blights a man's purpose and shortens his aim.
Despise it with all of your hatred of error;
   Refuse it the lodgment it seeks in your brain;

Arm against it as a creature of terror,
 And all that you dream of you some day shall gain.

Can't is the word that is foe to ambition,
 An enemy ambushed to shatter your will;
Its prey is forever the man with a mission
 And bows but to courage and patience and skill.
Hate it, with hatred that's deep and undying,
 For once it is welcomed 'twill break any man;
Whatever the goal you are seeking, keep trying
 And answer this demon by saying: "I can."

—EDGAR A. GUEST

Voluntary habit-building is self-discipline in
its highest and noblest form of application.

—NAPOLEON HILL

We shape our future through our actions. How are you designing yours?

Today

I shall do so much in the years to come,
But what have I done today?
I shall give out gold in princely sum,
But what did I give today?
I shall lift the heart and dry the tear
I shall plant a hope in the place of fear
I shall speak with words of love and cheer,
But what have I done today?
I shall bring to each lonely life a smile
But give to truth a greater birth
And to steadfast faith a deeper worth,
I shall feed the hungering souls of earth,
But whom have I fed today?

—ANONYMOUS

I can't believe what you say unless it
harmonizes with what you do.
—NAPOLEON HILL

A task once begun is nearly done.

Lose the Day Loitering

Lose the day loitering, 'twill be the same story
To-morrow, and the next more dilatory,
For indecision brings its own delays,
And days are lost lamenting o'er lost days.
Are you in earnest? Seize this very minute!
What you can do, or think you can, begin it!
Only engage, and then the mind grows heated;
Begin it, and the work will be completed.

–JOHANN WOLFGANG VON GOETHE

The more you supervise yourself the less
you will have to be supervised by others.

–NAPOLEON HILL

Simply put, there is no can't!

It Couldn't Be Done

Somebody said that it couldn't be done,
    But he with a chuckle replied
That "maybe it couldn't," but he would be one
    Who wouldn't say so till he'd tried.
So he buckled right in with the trace of a grin
    On his face. If he worried he hid it.
He started to sing as he tackled the thing
    That couldn't be done, and he did it.

Somebody scoffed: "Oh, you'll never do that;
    At least no one ever had done it";
But he took off his coat and he took off his hat,
    And the first thing we knew he'd begun it.
With a lift of his chin and a bit of a grin,
    Without any doubting or quiddit,
He started to sing as he tackled the thing
    That couldn't be done, and he did it.

There are thousands to tell you it cannot be done,
    There are thousands to prophesy failure;
There are thousands to point out to you, one by one,
    The dangers that wait to assail you.
But just buckle in with a bit of a grin,
    Just take off you coat and go to it;

Just start to sing as you tackle the thing
    That "cannot be done," and you'll do it.

–EDGAR A. GUEST

Successful men move on their own initiative but
they know where they are going before they start.

–NAPOLEON HILL

One step at a time is the surest way to proceed to your destination. There are no shortcuts.

Two Raindrops

(A Fable)

Two little raindrops were born in a shower,
And one was so pompously proud of his power,
He got in his head an extravagant notion
He'd hustle right off and swallow the ocean.
A blade of grass that grew by the brook
Called for a drink, but no notice he took
Of such trifling things. He must hurry to be
Not a mere raindrop, but the whole sea.
A stranded ship needed water to float,
But he could not bother to help a boat.
He leaped in the sea with a puff and a blare—
And nobody ever knew he was there!

But the other drop as along it went
Found the work to do for which it was sent:
It refreshed the lily that drooped its head,
And bathed the grass that was almost dead.
It got under the ships and helped them along,
And all the while sang a cheerful song.
It worked every step of the way it went,
Bringing joy to others, to itself content.
At last it came to its journey's end,
And welcomed the sea as an old-time friend.
"An ocean," it said, "there could not be
Except for the millions of drops like me."

                                    —JOSEPH MORRIS

❧❧

A "swelled head" doesn't always indicate
a surplus of brains.

–NAPOLEON HILL

In your hurry to create a successful life, don't miss the life you have been given.

My Own Shall Come to Me

Serene, I fold my hands and wait,
Nor care for wind, or tide, or sea;
I rave no more 'gainst Time or Fate,
For, lo! my own shall come to me.

I stay my haste, I make delays,
For what avails this eager pace?
I stand amid the eternal ways,
And what is mine shall know my face.

Asleep, awake, by night or day,
The friends I seek are seeking me,
No wind can drive my bark astray,
Nor change the tide of destiny.

What matter if I stand alone?
I wait with joy the coming years;
My heart shall reap where it has sown,
And garner up its fruit of tears.

The waters know their own and draw
The brook that springs in yonder height;
So flows the good with equal law
Until the soul of pure delight. . . .

The stars come nightly to the sky;
The tidal wave unto the sea;
Nor time, nor space, nor deep, nor high,
Can keep my own away from me.

–JOHN BURROUGHS

The smart man sees to it that his head
and heart pull together.

–NAPOLEON HILL

7

Poems of Accurate Thinking

Thinking accurately requires the use of self-discipline and controlled attention. It is an essential component to success because it requires a person to not jump to conclusions, to not choose sides without thinking, and to continually ask the telling question, "How do you know?" When decisions seem a breeze, we are probably not putting accurate thought behind our mental processes but rather allowing our emotions to control our thinking. Decisions based solely on emotions can have disastrous effects. Recalling that life is a composite portrait of what we have thought and the actions we have taken, surely we can realize the strong position accurate thinking has in the ultimate outcome of our lives. Spend some time utilizing accurate thinking, and spend less time in regret.

—Judith Williamson

From the Writings of Dr. Napoleon Hill:

Accurate thinking demands keen judgment. You must, for example, learn to distinguish between hard facts and hearsay, between the important and the unimportant, between the pertinent and the impertinent.

It is important, too, that you arrive at your decisions through reason, rather than emotion. Fear, love, anger, jealousy, revenge, vanity, and greed have no place in accurate thinking.

Those who lead humanity to greater heights of achievement are the lonely souls who refuse to let others do their thinking for them, who aren't afraid of new and startling ideas, who insist on making their own decisions and forming their own opinions.

The man who understands how to reach decisions intelligently is not only the master of his own destiny, but he may also control the destinies of many others. Let us, therefore, analyze the principle through which decisions may be reached intelligently, viz:

1. Before reaching a decision be sure you have at hand all the facts available in connection with, or affecting that decision.

2. Learn to distinguish the difference between facts and mere hearsay, even though some effort may be required to separate the two.

3. Learn to make a distinction between important and unimportant facts.

4. When it is impossible to avail yourself of all the facts you need in making a decision, use your past experience and your common sense and supply theory for the missing facts. All decisions reached in this way should be made with mental reservations and should be subject to immediate change if later it is discovered that the assumed facts were not correct.

Avoid unnecessary detours by following the rules of the road.

Four Things

Four things a man must learn to do
If he would make his record true:
To think without confusion clearly;
To love his fellow-men sincerely;
To act from honest motives purely;
To trust in God and Heaven securely.

–HENRY VAN DYKE

Learn the difference between being smart and
being wise and you will have more knowledge than
many who believe that they are highly educated.

–NAPOLEON HILL

Just begin it and the means to finish it will appear.

Start Where You Stand

Start where you stand and never mind the past,
   The past won't help you in beginning new,
If you have left it all behind at last
   Why, that's enough, you're done with it, you're through;
This is another chapter in the book,
   This is another race that you have planned,
Don't give the vanished days a backward look,
   Start where you stand.

The world won't care about your old defeats
   If you can start anew and win success,
The future is your time, and time is fleet
   And there is much of work and strain and stress;
Forget the buried woes and dead despairs,
   Here is a brand new trial right at hand,
The future is for him who does and dares,
   Start where you stand.

Old failures will not halt, old triumphs aid,
   To-day's the thing, to-morrow soon will be;
Get in the fight and face it unafraid,
   And leave the past to ancient history;
What has been, has been; yesterday is dead
   And by it you are neither blessed nor banned,
Take courage, man, be brave and drive ahead,
   Start where you stand.

                                   –BERTON BRALEY

Opportunity generally takes up with
the man who first recognizes it.

–NAPOLEON HILL

If everything seems to be going in the wrong direction, it is time to turn your canoe around.

The World Is Against Me

"The world is against me," he said with a sigh.
"Somebody stops every scheme that I try.
The world has me down and it's keeping me there;
I don't get a chance. Oh, the world is unfair!
When a fellow is poor then he can't get a show;
The world is determined to keep him down low."

"What of Abe Lincoln? I asked. "Would you say
That he was much richer than you are to-day?
He hadn't your chance of making his mark,
And his outlook was often exceedingly dark;
Yet he clung to his purpose with courage most grim
And he got to the top. Was the world against him?

"What of Ben Franklin? I've oft heard it said
That many a time he went hungry to bed.
He started with nothing but courage to climb,
But patiently struggled and waited his time.
He dangled awhile from real poverty's limb,
Yet he got to the top. Was the world against him?

"I could name you a dozen, yes, hundreds, I guess
Of poor boys who've patiently climbed to success;
All boys who were down and who struggled alone,

Who'd have thought themselves rich if your fortune
  they'd known;
yet they rose in the world you're so quick to condemn,
And I'm asking you now, was the world against them?"

–EDGAR A. GUEST

The only real limitation of the human mind is
that which a man sets up in his own mind.

–NAPOLEON HILL

Right thinking leads a person to right living. Right living always leads to success.

If

If you can keep your head when all about you
    Are losing theirs and blaming it on you,
If you can trust yourself when all men doubt you,
    But make allowance for their doubting too;
If you can wait and not be tired by waiting,
    Or being lied about, don't deal in lies,
Or being hated don't give way to hating,
    And yet don't look too good, nor talk too wise:

If you can dream—and not make dreams your master;
    If you can think—and not make thoughts your aim,
If you can meet with Triumph and Disaster
    And treat those two imposters just the same;
If you can bear to hear the truth you've spoken
    Twisted by knaves to make a trap for fools,
Or watch the things you gave your life to, broken,
    And stoop and build 'em up with worn-out tools:

If you can make one heap of all your winnings
    And risk it on one turn of pitch-and-toss,
And lose, and start again at your beginnings
    And never breathe a word about your loss;
If you can force your heart and nerve and sinew
    To serve your turn long after they are gone,

And so hold on when there is nothing in you
    Except the Will which say to them: "Hold on!"

If you can talk with crowds and keep your virtue,
    Or walk with Kings—nor lose the common touch,
If neither foes nor loving friends can hurt you,
    If all men count with you, but none too much;
If you can fill the unforgiving minute
    With sixty seconds' worth of distance run,
Yours is the Earth and everything that's in it,
    And—which is more—you'll be a Man, my son!

                 –RUDYARD KIPLING

A man needs to be always on guard, not so
much against the danger from others as the
dangers of his own judgment.
        –NAPOLEON HILL

Little successes should not make a big fool out of you. Ration your self-praise.

Swellitis

Somebody said he'd done it well,
And presto! his head began to swell;
Bigger and bigger the poor thing grew—
A wonder it didn't split in two.
In size a balloon could scarcely match it;
He needed a fishing-pole to scratch it;--
But six and a half was the size of his hat,
And it rattled around on his head at that!

"Good work," somebody chanced to say,
And his chest swelled big as a load of hay.
About himself, like a rooster, he crowed;
Of his wonderful work he bragged and blowed.
He marched around with a peacock strut;
Gigantic to him was the figure he cut;--
But he wore a very small-sized suit,
And loosely it hung on him, to boot!

HE was the chap who made things hum!
HE was the drumstick and the drum!
HE was the shirt bosom and the starch!
HE was the keystone in the arch!
HE was the axis of the earth!
Nothing existed before his birth!

But when he was off from work a day,
Nobody knew that he was away!

This is a fact that is sad to tell:
It's the empty head that is bound to swell;
It's the light-weight fellow who soars to the skies,
And bursts like a bubble before your eyes.
A big man is humbled by honest praise,
And tries to think of all the ways
To improve his work and do it well;--
But a little man starts of himself to yell!

–JOSEPH MORRIS

If your employer doesn't see all your good qualities,
perhaps it's because they are not as pronounced
as you think they are.

–NAPOLEON HILL

All the riches in the world cannot buy one sunrise or one sunset.
Count your blessings.

The Millionaire

I've got my name on the river,
I've got my name on the sea,
I've got my name on the summer skies,
They all belong to me.

I've got my name on the violets
That grow in their corner fair,
And wherever Nature has planted peace,
My name is written there.

As far as the eye can travel,
From where I stand in the sun,
I've got my name on the things I see
And I own them, every one!

I've got my name on the singing birds
That mate when spring is new;
But I won't be selfish with all the things—
I'll share them, my friend, with you!

There is no deed to the river,
There is no lock to the sea;
Not all the power in all the world
Can take take their joy from me!

There is no fence round the Heavens,
No vault holds the sunset's gold;
The earth is mine and the
Heavens are mine,
Till all the suns grow cold.

The stars are my thousand jewels,
And *Life* is my bread and wine,
And all that I see was made for me,
And all that I love, is mine!

–ANONYMOUS

Your life and your world are what you make
them by your thoughts and deeds.
–NAPOLEON HILL

If gold is the treasure you seek, make certain that you have an accurate treasure map to follow.

Eldorado

Gaily bedight,
A gallant knight,
In sunshine and in shadow,
Had journeyed long,
Singing a song,
In search of Eldorado.

But he grew old—
This knight so bold—
And o'er his heart a shadow
Fell, as he found
No spot of ground
That looked like Eldorado.

And, as his strength
Failed him at length,
He met a pilgrim shadow—
"Shadow," said he,
"Where can it be—
This land of Eldorado?"

"Over the Mountains
Of the Moon,
Down the Valley of the Shadow,

Ride, boldly ride,"
The shade replied,
"If you seek for Eldorado!"

−EDGAR ALLAN POE

Thinking my way through problems is
safer than wishing my way through.

−NAPOLEON HILL

Wishing lulls one into thought that is more like a lullaby than a standing ovation.

Star Light, Star Bright

Star light, star bright,
First star I see tonight,
I wish I may, I wish I might,
Have the wish I wish tonight.

–ANONYMOUS

Hopeful wishing is a good starter, but a poor finisher.
–NAPOLEON HILL

8

Poems of Teamwork

Teamwork is a blessing for all members of the team. When individuals work voluntarily in cooperation toward a designated goal, everyone shares the burden, accountability, and ultimately recognition. As efforts are coordinated and responsibility is taken, team members accomplish tasks efficiently. The acronym TEAM—Together Everyone Achieves More—says it all.

—Judith Williamson

From the Writings of Dr. Napoleon Hill:

Cooperation is something like love. You can't buy it. You must earn it. Whether a person is a job-holder or the head of a plant, he must have the friendly cooperation of the people with whom he works.

Regardless of your calling, to get the friendly cooperation of others you must find ways to instill in them the urgent desire to help you.

Nothing ever "just happens." Someone has to make things happen.

Teamwork and the Golden Rule go hand in hand. It is the application of the Golden Rule that brings benefits. These benefits are so numerous and varied that they touch life through almost every human relationship. The following are some of the more important benefits of applying the Golden Rule:

1. Opens the mind for the guidance of Infinite Intelligence, through faith.

2. Develops self-reliance, through a better relationship with one's conscience.

3. Builds a sound character sufficient to sustain one in times of emergency. Develops a more attractive personality.

4. Attracts the friendly cooperation of others in all human relationships.

5. Discourages unfriendly opposition from others.

6. Gives one peace of mind and freedom from self- established limitations.

7. Gives one immunity against the more damaging forms of fear, since the man with a clear conscience seldom fears anything or anyone.

8. Enables one to go to prayer with clean hands and a clear heart.

9. Attracts favorable opportunities for self-promotion in one's occupation, business or profession.

10. Eliminates the desire for something for nothing.

11. Makes the rendering of useful service a joy that can be had in no other way.

12. Provides one with an influential reputation for honesty and fair dealing, which is the basis of all confidence.

13. Serves as a discouragement to the slanderer and a reprimand to the thief.

14. Makes one a power for good, by example, wherever he comes into contact with others.

15. Discourages all the baser instincts of greed and envy and revenge, and gives wings to the higher instincts of love and fellowship.

16. Brings one within easy communicating distance of the Creator, through the medium of an undisturbed mind.

17. Enables one to recognize the joys of accepting the truth that every man is, and by right should be, his brother's keeper.

18. Establishes a deeper personal spirituality.

Instead of pushing a rope to no avail, why not pull it together?

Co-Operation

It ain't the guns nor armament,
    Nor funds that they can pay,
But the close co-operation,
    That makes them win the day.

It ain't the individual
    Nor the army as a whole,
But the everlasting team-work
    Of every bloomin' soul.

–J. MASON KNOX

I cannot succeed and remain successful
without the friendly cooperation of others.

–NAPOLEON HILL

You can learn and contribute a great deal by being versatile.

Preparedness

For all your days prepare,
   And meet them ever alike:
When you are the anvil, bear—
   When you are the hammer, strike.

—EDWIN MARKHAM

The sure way to promote yourself
is to help others get ahead.

—NAPOLEON HILL

Strive to be the very best at whatever you are assigned to do at the moment. If you do, your next assignment might just be a promotion!

Be the Best of Whatever You Are

If you can't be a pine on the top of the hill
    Be a scrub in the valley—but be
The best little scrub by the side of the rill;
    Be a bush if you can't be a tree.

If you can't be a bush be a bit of the grass,
    And some highway some happier make;
If you can't be a muskie then just be a bass—
    But the liveliest bass in the lake!

We can't all be captains, we've got to be crew,
    There's something for all of us here.
There's big work to do and there's lesser to do,
    And the task we must do is the near.

If you can't be a highway then just be a trail,
    If you can't be the sun be a star;
It isn't by size that you win or you fail—
    Be the best of whatever you are!

                         –DOUGLAS MALLOCH

It will be a great day in your life when you
learn to stop kicking and start pulling.
–NAPOLEON HILL

9

Poems of Adversity and Defeat

Many individuals are drawn to the study of Dr. Hill's philosophy after they experience an adversity or defeat. These setbacks in life cause people to sit up and take notice concerning where their life is headed. When unwanted things occur, people seek out better methods for reaching their dreams or their life's purpose. Dr. Hill acknowledges that setbacks can be a good tool for advancement because when a person experiences adversity there is also buried within the adversity a seed for an equal or equivalent benefit. The difficult part is discovering what exactly that seed is, and when found caring for it with the concern one devotes to a newborn. Remember, it is an acorn not a full grown oak tree that one discovers. Nurture the seedling, encourage it to sprout, celebrate its growth, and proclaim its maturity. Growth is a process that takes a great deal of effort. Just ask anyone who has grown an oak tree!

—Judith Williamson

From the Writings of Dr. Napoleon Hill:

Accurate analysis of more than one thousand men and women in the upper brackets of success, in a variety of callings, revealed the astounding fact that in each individual the success attained was in almost exact proportion to the adversities and defeats which had been met with and overcome.

Go backward into your own past experiences of adversity and you may observe that the passing of time has proved that some of your failures and defeats were only blessings in disguise. It is often difficult to find the seed of an equivalent benefit when you are too close to the wound of an unpleasant circumstance, but TIME, the great universal healer, often reveals this seed and converts it into a priceless asset.

When you are faced with a problem that needs a solution, regardless of how perplexing it may be:

1. Ask for Divine Guidance. Ask for help in finding the right solution.

2. Think.

3. State the problem. Analyze and define it.

4. State to *yourself* enthusiastically: "That's good!"

5. Ask yourself some specific questions, such as:
   a. What's good about it?
   b. How can I turn this adversity into a seed of equivalent or greater benefit; or how can I turn this liability into a greater asset?

6. Keep searching for answers to these questions until you find at least one answer that *can work*.

Quitting is not an option for those who are serious about success.

Don't Quit

When things go wrong, as they sometimes will,
When the road you're trudging seems all up hill,
When the funds are low and the debts are high,
And you want to smile, but you have to sigh,
When care is pressing you down a bit,
Rest, if you must—but don't you quit.

Life is queer with its twists and turns,
As everyone of us sometimes learns,
And many a failure turns about
When he might have won had he stuck it out;
Don't give up, though the pace seems slow—
You might succeed with another blow.

Often the goal is nearer than
It seems to a faint and faltering man,
Often the struggler has given up
When he might have captured the victor's cup.
And he learned too late, when the night slipped down,
How close he was to the golden crown.

Success is failure turned inside out—
The silver tint of the clouds of doubt—
And you never can tell how close your are,
It may be near when it seems afar;

So stick to the fight when you're hardest hit—
It's when things seem worst that you mustn't quit.

–UNKNOWN

Don't fear defeat. It may reveal to you
powers you didn't know you possessed.

–NAPOLEON HILL

Surrender and you are labeled a failure, persist and you are labeled a success. What do you want to be called?

Never Give Up!

Never give up! If adversity presses,
Providence wisely has mingled the cup,
And the best counsel, in all your distresses,
Is the stout watchword of "Never give up."

—MARTIN F. TUPPER

Victory is always possible for the person
who refuses to stop fighting.

—NAPOLEON HILL

Opportunity is always in full view. You just need to focus to see it.

Opportunity

They do me wrong who say I come no more
    When once I knock and fail to find you in;
For every day I stand outside your door,
    And bid you wake, and rise to fight and win.

Wail not for precious chances passed away,
    Weep not for golden ages on the wane!
Each night I burn the records of the day,—
    At sunrise every soul is born again!

Laugh like a boy at splendors that have sped,
    To vanished joys be blind and deaf and dumb;
My judgments seal the dead past with its dead,
    But never bind a moment yet to come.

Though deep in mire, wring not your hands and weep;
    I lend my arm to all who say "I can!"
No shame-faced outcast ever sank so deep,
    But yet might rise and be again a man!

Dost thou behold thy lost youth all aghast?
    Dost reel from righteous Retribution's blow?
Then turn from blotted archives of the past,
    And find the future's pages white as snow.

Art thou a mourner? Rouse thee from thy spell;
Art thou a sinner? Sins may be forgiven;
Each morning gives thee wings to flee from hell,
Each night a star to guide thy feet to heaven.

–WALTER MALONE

Failure comes from drifting,
success from persistent climbing.

–NAPOLEON HILL

Knowing that there is a point "A" and a point "B" is the hard part. Getting from one to the other requires commitment, but not genius. There is always a way.

If You Can't Go Over Or Under, Go Round

A baby mole got to feeling big,
And wanted to show how he could dig;
So he plowed along in the soft, warm dirt
Till he hit something hard, and it surely hurt!
A dozen stars flew out of his snout;
He sat on his haunches, began to pout;
Then rammed the thing again with his head—
His grandpap picked him up half dead,
"Young man," he said, "though your pate is bone,
You can't butt your way through solid stone.
This bit of advice is good, I've found:
If you can't go over or under, go round."

A traveler came to a stream one day,
And because it presumed to cross his way,
And wouldn't turn round to suit his whim
And change its course to go with him,
His anger rose far more than it should,
And he vowed he'd cross right where he stood.
A man said there was a bridge below,
But not a step would he budge or go.

The current was swift and the bank was steep,
But he jumped right in with a violent leap.
A fisherman dragged him out half-drowned:
"When you can't go over or under, go round."

If you come to a place that you can't get *through*
Or *over* or *under*, the thing to do
Is to find a way *round* the impassable wall,
Not say you'll go YOUR way or not at all.
You can always get to the place you're going,
If you'll set your sails as the wind is blowing.
If the mountains are high, go round the valley;
If the streets are blocked, go up some alley;
If the parlor-car's filled, don't scorn a freight;
If the front door's closed, go in the side gate.
To reach your goal this advice is sound:
If you can't go over or under, go round."

–JOSEPH MORRIS

Temporary loss often results in permanent gain.

–NAPOLEON HILL

Look for the opportunity buried within the adversity. Unearth it, and you will be headed for the winner's circle.

The Uncommon Man

I do not choose to be a common man. It is my right to be uncommon if I can. I seek opportunity—not security. I do not wish to be a kept citizen, humbled, dulled, by having the State look after me.

I want to take the calculated risk; to dream and to build; to fail or succeed. I refuse to barter incentive to a dole. I prefer the challenges of life to the guaranteed existence; the thrill of fulfillment to the calm state of Utopia.

I will not trade freedom for beneficence nor my dignity for a handout. I will never cower before any master nor bend to any threat. It is my heritage to stand erect, proud and unafraid; to think and act for myself; to enjoy the benefits of my creation, and to face the world boldly and say—This I have done!

–ANONYMOUS

Some men have learned to use the
winds of adversity to sail their ship of life.
–NAPOLEON HILL

Struggle strengthens a person for what comes next.

The Struggle

Did you ever want to take your two bare hands,
    And choke out of the world your big success?
Beat, torn fists bleeding, pathways rugged, grand,
    By sheer brute strength and bigness, nothing less?
So at the last, triumphant, battered, strong,
    You might gaze down on what you choked and beat,
And say, "Ah, world, you've wrought to do me wrong;
    And thus have I accepted my defeat."

Have you ever dreamed of virile deeds, and vast,
    And then come back from dreams with wobbly knees,
To find your way (the braver vision past),
    By picking meekly at typewriter keys;
By bending o'er a ledger, day by day,
    By some machine-like drudging? No great woe
To grapple with. Slow, painful is the way,
    And still, the bravest fight and conquer so.

–MIRIAM TEICHNER

I can promote myself to almost any position I desire by
the simple process of getting myself ready to fill the job.

–NAPOLEON HILL

Without sorrow we cannot experience joy. How would you measure one without the other?

Life's Lesson

I learn as the years roll onward
  And I leave the past behind,
That much I have counted sorrow
  But proves that God is kind;
That many a flower I'd long for
  Had hidden a thorn of pain,
And many a rugged by-path
  Led to fields of ripened grain.

The clouds that cover the sunshine,
  They cannot banish the sun,
And the earth shines out the brighter
  When the weary rain is done.
We must stand in the deepest shadow
  To see the clearest light;
And often through Wrong's own darkness
  Comes the weary strength of Right.

The sweetest rest is at even,
  After a wearisome day,
When the heavy burden of labor
  Has been borne from our hearts away;
And those who have never known sorrow
  Cannot know the infinite peace

That falls on the troubled spirit
When it sees at last release.

We must live through the dreary Winter
If we would value the Spring;
And the woods must be cold and silent
Before the robins sing.
The flowers must be buried in darkness
Before they can bud and bloom,
And the sweetest, warmest sunshine
Comes after the storm and gloom.

—ANONYMOUS

Failure seems to be Nature's plan for
preparing men for great responsibilities.
—NAPOLEON HILL

Failure after failure without self-analysis has never primed a soul
for success.

Life

All in the dark we grope along,
  And if we go amiss
We learn at least which path is wrong,
  And there is gain in this.

We do not always win the race
  By only running right,
We have to tread the mountain's base
  Before we reach its height.

But he who loves himself the last
  And knows the use of pain,
Though strewn with errors all his past,
  He surely shall attain.

Some souls there are that needs must taste
  Of wrong, ere choosing right;
We should not call those years a waste
  Which led us to the light.

                    —ELLA WHEELER WILCOX

Many men have found opportunities in failure
and adversity which they could not recognize
in the more favorable circumstances.

–NAPOLEON HILL

Bad times are trying, but not everlasting.

This, Too, Shall Pass Away

Art thou in misery, brother?   Then I pray
Be comforted.   Thy grief shall pass away.
Art thou elated?   Ah, be not too gay;
Temper thy joy: this, too, shall pass away.
Art thou in danger?   Still let reason sway,
And cling to hope: this, too, shall pass away.
Temped art thou?   In all thine anguish lay
One truth to heart: this, too, shall pass away.
Do rays of loftier glory round thee play?
Kinglike art thou?   This, too, shall pass away!
Whate'er thou art, where'er thy footsteps stray,
Heed these wise words: This, too, shall pass away.

—PAUL HAMILTON HAYNE

During the days of plenty remember
the coming days of want.

—NAPOLEON HILL

10

Poems of Cosmic Habitforce

Cosmic Habitforce is the term used to describe the natural laws of the universe in operation. This sounds very scientific and not directly related to the study of success, however as you will begin to understand, it is at the very heart of the matter. Napoleon Hill reminds us that we are a part of the universe and not apart from it. Therefore, we are subject to and under the control of all the universal laws that operate all around us. Because we are part of creation we are not exempt from these laws but subservient to them. Dr. Hill's good news message is that if we work in tandem with these universal laws, we will achieve our definiteness of purpose much sooner. Opposition only creates undue struggle. Habits are ways that we either conform to or resist these universal laws. You've probably heard the saying that actions create our habits, habits create our character, and character creates our destiny. This is true especially in the light of Cosmic Habitforce. Recognize your control over the habits you create, create only those that further your purpose, and then proceed to reap your reward. It's as natural as that!

—Judith Williamson

From the Writings of Dr. Napoleon Hill:

We are what we are because of the habits we live by each day. Habits are of two types—those we deliberately cultivate to attain definite desired ends, and those which fasten themselves upon us as a result of circumstances we do not try to avoid or control.

Voluntary habits which we set up in our own minds and express repeatedly through our words and deeds are the only dependable means of insuring success in any calling.

A "planned" life is the only successful way to make life pay off on one's own terms. Every successful career needs the same planning, the same budgeting of time, energy and money, that goes into a successful business enterprise.

Generally speaking there are two types of minds—the type which has been conditioned to believe in success, to demand it, and usually finds it; and the type which, by neglect in the formation of a success consciousness, has been conditioned to expect poverty and failure, and usually finds these.

First of all, you should know that this law is the climax of the entire philosophy of individual achievement. To get a slight degree of understanding of the importance of this law, consider the fact that it is the Master Key to the principles previously described, and its benefits are available only to those who master and apply the instructions in previous chapters.

Understanding and application of the law can release you from fears and self-imposed limitations, thus enabling you to take full possession of your own mind! If it offered no further promise this would be sufficient to justify all the time you may devote to its study.

It can help you attain economic freedom for life provided you follow the instructions in the previous chapters.

It can aid you in eliminating the opposition of others in all your relationships, thus enabling you to negotiate your way through life with a minimum of friction.

It can help you master most, if not all, of the major causes of physical conditions that cause illness and disease.

It can clear your mind of negative conditions, thus paving the way for that state of mind known as faith.

Cosmic Habitforce is the particular application of energy with which nature maintains the existing relationship between the atoms of matter, the stars and planets, the seasons of the year, night and day, sickness and health, life and death, and more important to us right now, it is the medium through which all habits and all human relationships are maintained, the medium through which thought is translated into its physical equivalent.

You, of course, know that nature maintains a perfect balance between all the elements of matter and energy throughout the universe. You can see the stars and planets move with perfect precision, each keeping its own place in Time and Space, year in and year out.

You can see the seasons of the year come and go with perfect regularity.

You can see that night and day follow each other in unending regularity.

You can see that an oak tree grows from an acorn and a pine grows from the seed of its ancestor. An acorn never produces a pine nor does a pine cone ever produce an oak, and nothing is ever produced that does not have its antecedents in something else which preceded it.

These are simple facts that anyone can see, but what most people cannot see or understand is the universal law through which nature maintains perfect balance between all matter and energy throughout the universe, forcing every living thing to reproduce itself.

Take time for yourself and the world will appear better too.

Cares

The little cares that fretted me,
   I lost them yesterday
Among the fields above the sea,
   Among the winds at play;
Among the lowing of the herds,
   The rustling of the trees,
Among the singing of the birds,
   The humming of the bees.

The foolish fears of what may happen,
   I cast them all away
Among the clover-scented grass,
   Among the new-mown hay;
Among the husking of the corn
   Where drowsy poppies nod,
Where ill thoughts die and good are born,
   Out in the fields with God.

—ELIZABETH BARRETT BROWNING

The greatest of all gifts is the gift of an
opportunity for one to help himself.

—NAPOLEON HILL

Thankfulness and gratitude bring joy to you too.

I'm Glad

I'm glad the sky is painted blue;
   And the earth is painted green;
And such fresh air
   All sandwiched in between.

–ANONYMOUS

Don't forget to express gratitude, daily, for the blessings you have, by prayer or affirmation.

–NAPOLEON HILL

Make time to take time for yourself.

No Time to Stand and Stare

What is this life if, full of care,
We have no time to stand and stare?

No time to stand beneath the boughs
And stare as long as sheep or cows:

No time to see, when woods we pass,
Where squirrels hid their nuts in grass:

No time to see, in broad daylight,
Streams full of stars, like skies at night:

A poor life this if, full of care,
We have no time to stand and stare.

—WILLIAM HENRY DAVIES

Men with positive mental attitudes
are never found in a rut.
—NAPOLEON HILL

Look for the good and you will always find it in abundance.

Pippa's Song

The year's at the spring
   And day's at the morn;
Morning's at seven;
The hillside's dew-pearled;
The lark's on the wing;
The snail's on the thorn;
God's in his heaven—
All's right with the world.

–ROBERT BROWNING

Go to bed praying and get up singing and notice
what a fine day's work you will do.

–NAPOLEON HILL

Life's beauties endure.

The Rainbow

My heart leaps up when I behold
A rainbow in the sky:
So was it when my life began;
So is it now I am a man;
So be it when I shall grow old,
Or let me die!
The Child is father of the Man;
And I could wish my days to be
Bound each to each by natural piety.

–WILLIAM WORDSWORTH

Some people accumulate money so they can convert it
into happiness, but the wiser ones accumulate happiness
so they can give it away and still have it in abundance.

–NAPOLEON HILL

Honor all creation.

Hurt No Living Thing

Hurt no living thing;
Ladybird, nor butterfly,
Nor moth with dusty wing,
Nor cricket chirping cheerily,
Nor grasshopper so light of leap,
Nor dancing gnat, nor beetle fat,
Nor harmless worms that creep.

–CHRISTINA ROSSETTI

All voluntary positive habits are the products of will
power directed toward the attainment of definite goals.

–NAPOLEON HILL

The memory of home endures for a lifetime.

No Place Like Home

'Mid pleasures and palaces though we may roam,
Be it ever so humble, there's no place like home;
A charm from the sky seems to hallow us there,
Which, seek through the world, is ne'er met with
    elsewhere.
       Home, home, sweet, sweet home!
There's no place like home, there's no place like home!

An exile from home, splendor dazzles in vain;
Oh, give me my lowly thatched cottage again!
The birds singing gaily, that came at my call—
Give me them—and the peace of mind, dearer than all!
       Home, home, sweet, sweet home!
There's no place like home, there's no place like home!

I gaze on the moor as I tread the drear wild,
And feel that my mother now thinks of her child,
As she looks on that moon from our own cottage door
Thro' the woodbine, whose fragrance shall cheer me no
    more.
       Home, home, sweet, sweet home!
There's no place like home, there's no place like home!

How sweet 'tis to sit 'neath a fond father's smile,
And the cares of a mother to soothe and beguile!
Let others delight 'mid new pleasures to roam,
But give me, oh, give me, the pleasures of home,
    Home, home, sweet, sweet home!
There's no place like home, there's no place like home!

To thee I'll return, overburdened with care;
The heart's dearest solace will smile on me there;
No more from that cottage again will I roam;
Be it ever so humble, there's no place like home.
    Home, home, sweet, sweet home!
There's no place like home, there's no place like home!
                –JOHN HOWARD PAYNE

Try to find the happy medium between
too much and too little of everything.
        –NAPOLEON HILL

Life reminds us that we are finite in body, infinite in spirit.

Life and Death

Life! I know not what thou art,
But know that thou and I must part;
And when, or how, or where we met
I own to me a secret yet.

Life! We've been long together,
Through pleasant and through cloudy weather;
'Tis hard to part when friends are dear;
Perhaps will cost a sigh, a tear;
    Then steal away, give little warning,
Choose thine own time;
Say not "Good Night"—but in some brighter clime,
    Bid me "Good Morning!"

–ANNA BARBAULD

The orderliness of the world of natural laws gives
evidence that they are under control of a universal plan.
–NAPOLEON HILL

Repetition creates a pattern for success.

Life

Forenoon and afternoon and night,—Forenoon,
And afternoon, and night,—Forenoon, and—what!
The empty song repeats itself. No more?
Yea, that is Life: make this forenoon sublime,
This afternoon a psalm, this night a prayer,
And Time is conquered, and thy crown is won.

—EDWARD ROWLAND SILL

All things tend toward equaling themselves,
one against its opposite, over a period of time.

–NAPOLEON HILL

Life's culmination is just like life's origin – nothing to fear.

Let Me But Live My Life From Year to Year

Let me but live my life from year to year,
  With forward face and unreluctant soul.
  Not hurrying to, nor turning from the goal;
Nor mourning for the things that disappear
In the dim past, nor holding back in fear
  From what the future veils; but with a whole
  And happy heart, that pays its toll
To youth and age, and travels on with cheer.

So let the way wind up the hill or down,
  O'er rough or smooth, the journey will be joy;
  Still seeking what I sought when but a boy,
New friendship, high adventure, and a crown,
  I shall grow old, but never lose life's zest,
  Because the road's last turn will be the best.

       –HENRY VAN DYKE

Anyone can quit when the going is hard,
but a thoroughbred never quits until he wins.

   –NAPOLEON HILL

11

Most Often Requested Reprints by Napoleon Hill

This final chapter will bring to your fingertips Dr. Hill's "poetic" writings. Although, Dr. Hill was not a poet, he did read many of the poems contained in this volume and even referred to them in his books. Poets like Edgar Guest, Ella Wheeler Wilcox, Jessie Rittenhouse, William Shakespeare, and Walter Wintle were Dr. Hill's favorites. He was inspired to write some of his most famous essays after reading these poems and more. Just for fun, see which poem reminds you of Dr. Hill's "Challenge to Life." It is in this volume.

As you read Dr. Hill's contributions, consider ways that you might relate the same things to a modern day reader. Jot a note to a friend, mentor a student, donate this volume to your local library, read the poems out loud to a study group, introduce Dr. Hill's success principles to a willing audience—in other words—do your part to make this world a better place in which to live. Don't let wonderful ideas like these rest on the shelves in libraries. Remember, the greatest intention is not worth the tiniest action. Baby steps can lead you to success. Take some now.

—Judith Williamson

Life and Success

Life is a series of ever-changing and shifting circumstances and experiences. No two experiences are alike. No two people are alike. Day after day we experience Life's kaleidoscopic changes. This makes it necessary for us to adapt ourselves to people who think and act in ways different from our own. Our success depends, very largely, upon how well we negotiate our way through these daily contacts with other people without friction or opposition.

A Challenge to Life

LIFE, you can't subdue me because I refuse to take your discipline too seriously.

When you try to hurt me I laugh, and laughter knows no pain. I appropriate your joys wherever I find them. Your sorrows neither discourage nor frighten me, for there is laughter in my soul.

Temporary defeat does not make me sad. I simply set music to the words of defeat and turn it into a song.

Your tears are not for me! I like laughter much better, and, because I like it, I use it as a substitute for grief and sorrow and pain and disappointment.

Life, you are a fickle trickster. Don't deny it.

You slipped the emotion of love into my heart so you might use it as a thorn with which to prick my soul, but I learned to dodge your trap—with laughter.

You try to lure me with the desire for gold, but I have fooled you by following the trail which leads to knowledge instead.

You induce me to build beautiful friendships, then convert my friends into enemies so you may harden my heart, but I side-step your fickleness by laughing off your attempt and selecting new friends in my own way.

You cause men to cheat me at trade so I will become distrustful, but I win again because I possess one precious asset which no man can steal—IT IS THE POWER TO THINK MY OWN THOUGHTS AND TO BE MYSELF.

You threaten me with death, but to me death is nothing worse than a long, peaceful sleep, and sleep is the sweetest of human experiences—excepting laughter.

You build the fire of hope in my breast, then sprinkle water on the flames, but I go you one better by rekindling the fire, and I laugh at you once more.

Life, you are licked as far as I am concerned because you have nothing with which to lure me away from laughter, and you are powerless to scare me into submission.

To a life of laughter, then, I raise my cup of cheer!

How would you like to become....

THE RICHEST MAN IN THE WORLD

THE RICHEST man in all the world lives over in Happy Valley.

He is rich in values that endure, in things he cannot lose—things that provide him with contentment, sound health, peace of mind and harmony within his soul.

Here is an inventory of his riches and how he acquired them:

"I found happiness by helping others to find it.

"I found sound health by living temperately and eating only the food my body requires to maintain itself.

"I am free from all causes and effects of fear and worry. "I hate no man, envy no man, but love and respect all mankind.

"I am engaged in a labor of love with which I mix play generously; therefore, I never grow tired.

"I pray daily, not for more riches, but for more vision with which to recognize, embrace and enjoy the great abundance of riches I already possess.

"I speak no name save only to honor it, and I slander no man for any cause whatsoever.

"I ask no favors of anyone except the privilege of sharing my blessings with all who desire them.

"I am on good terms with my conscience, therefore, it guides me accurately in everything I do.

"I have no enemies because I injure no man. Rather, I try to help everyone with whom I come in contact.

"I have more material wealth than I need because I am free from greed and covet only those things I can use constructively while I live. My wealth comes from those whom I have benefited by sharing my blessings.

"The estate of Happy Valley which I own is not taxable.

It exists mainly in my own mind, in intangible riches that cannot be assessed for taxation or appropriated except by those who adopt my way of life. I created this estate over a lifetime of effort by observing nature's law and forming habits to conform with them."

There are no copyrights on the Happy Valley Man's success creed.

If you will adopt it, and live by it, you can make life pay off on your own terms.

It can attract to you new and more desirable friends, as well as disarm enemies.

It can help you to occupy more space in the world and get more joy from living.

It can bring prosperity to your business, profession or calling, and make your home a paradise of profound enjoyment for every member of your family.

It can add years to your life and give you freedom from fear and anxiety.

It can help you to count your blessings and give you a greater appreciation of the things in life that really matter.

But above all, the Happy Valley Man's creed can bring you wisdom to solve all your personal problems—before they arise—and give you peace and contentment.

My Code of Ethics

I. I believe in the Golden Rule as the basis of all human conduct; therefore, I will never do to another person that which I would not be willing for that person to do to me if our positions were reversed.

II. I will be honest, even to the slightest detail, in all my transactions with others, not only because of my desire to be fair with them, but because of my desire to impress the idea of honesty on my own subconscious mind, thereby weaving this essential quality into my own character.

III. I will forgive those who are unjust toward me, with no thought as to whether they deserve it or not, because I understand the law through which forgiveness of others strengthens my own character and wipes out the effects of my own transgressions in my subconscious mind.

IV. I will be just, generous and fair with others always— even though I know that these acts will go unnoticed and unrewarded in the ordinary terms of reward— because I understand that one's own character is but the sum total of one's own acts and deeds.

V. Whatever time I may have to devote to the discovery and exposure of the weaknesses and faults of others I will devote, more profitably, to the discovery and correction of my own.

VI.   I will slander no person—no matter how much I may
      believe another person may deserve it—because I wish
      to plant no destructive suggestions in my own mind.

VII. I recognize the power of thought as being an inlet
      leading into my brain from the universal ocean of
      life; therefore, I will set no destructive thoughts afloat
      upon that ocean lest they pollute the minds of others.

VIII. I will conquer the common human tendency toward
      hatred, and envy, and selfishness, and jealousy, and
      malice, and pessimism, and doubt, and fear—for I
      believe these to be the seeds from which the world har-
      vests most of its troubles.

IX.   When my mind is not occupied with thoughts that
      tend toward the attainment of my definite goal in life, I
      will voluntarily keep it filled with thoughts of courage,
      self-confidence, good-will toward others, faith, kind-
      ness, loyalty, love for truth, and justice—for I believe
      these to be the seeds from which the world reaps its
      harvest of progressive growth.

X.   Because I know that my character is developed from
      my own acts and thoughts, I will guard with care all
      that goes into its development.

XII. Because I realize that enduring happiness comes only
      through helping others find it, and that no act of kind-
      ness is without its reward, even though it may never be
      directly repaid, I will do my best to assist others when
      and where the opportunity appears.

My Daily Creed

1. I know that I have the ability to achieve the object of my definite major purpose in life: Therefore, I DEMAND of myself persistent, continuous action toward its attainment, and I here and now promise to render such action.

2. I realize the dominating thoughts of my mind will eventually reproduce themselves in outward, physical action, and gradually transform themselves into physical reality: Therefore, I will concentrate my thoughts for thirty minutes daily upon the task of thinking of the person I intend to become, thereby creating in my mind a clear mental picture of that person.

3. I know that through the principle of auto-suggestion, any desire I persistently hold in my mind will eventually seek expression through some practical means of attaining the object back of it: Therefore, I will devote ten minutes daily to demanding of myself the development of unconditional self-reliance.

4. I have clearly written down a description of my definite chief aim in life, and I will never stop trying until I shall have developed sufficient self-reliance for its attainment in full.

5. I fully realize that no wealth or position of benefit can long endure unless built upon truth and justice: Therefore, I will engage in no transaction, in no human rela-

tionship, which does not benefit all whom it affects. I will succeed by attracting to myself the forces I wish to use and the cooperation of other people. I will induce others to serve me because of my willingness to serve others. I will cause others to believe in me because I will believe in them and in myself.

6. I will sign my name to this formula, commit it to memory, and repeat it aloud at least once daily, with full faith that it will gradually influence my thoughts and actions, so that I will become self-reliant and successful.

Countersigned: Signed:

*Maybe you, too, will meet the person that's holding
you back when you . . .*

Look In The Mirror

MY SECRETARY walked into my office early one morning and announced that a tramp was outside with an urgent
request that I see him. At first I decided to save time by send-
ing him the price of a sandwich and a cup of coffee, but something prompted me to have him sent in.

I've never seen a more dilapidated looking man. He had a
week's growth of beard and wrinkled clothes that looked as if
he had dragged them from a rag pile.

"I don't blame you for looking surprised at my appearance"
he began, "but I'm afraid you have me all wrong. I didn't come
to see you for a handout. I came to ask you to help me save my
life.

"My troubles began a year ago when I had a break with
my wife, and we were divorced. Then everything began to go
against me. I lost my business, and now I'm losing my health.

"I came to see you at the suggestion of a policeman who
stopped me just as I was going to jump in the river. He gave me
my choice of coming to see you or going to jail. He's waiting
outside to see that I carry out my promise."

The tone of the man's voice and the language he used indi-
cated clearly that he was a man of considerable education.

Questioning brought out the fact that he had owned one of
the best known restaurants in Chicago. I remembered seeing a
news account of it being sold at a sheriff's sale several months
previously.

I had my secretary get him a breakfast because he hadn't
eaten for two days. While the food was being prepared I got

the man's entire life story. Not once did he blame anyone for his condition but himself. That was a sign in his favor and one that gave me my cue as to how I could help him.

After he finished eating I did the talking.

"My friend," I began, "I have listened to your story very carefully and I'm deeply impressed by it. I am especially impressed with the fact that you haven't tried to alibi yourself clear of responsibility for your condition.

"I'm also impressed by the fact that you don't place blame on your former wife for your divorce. You are to be commended for speaking of her in the respectful way that you have."

By this time the man's spirits were rising higher and higher.

The moment had come for me to spring my plan of action and I let him have it in a way that made it register as I had hoped it would.

"You came to me for help" I continued, "but I am sorry to tell you that after hearing your story there is not one thing I can do to help you!"

"But," I continued, "I know a man who can help you if he will do it. He is here in this building right now and I will introduce you to him if you wish me to do so."

Then I took him by the arm and led him into my private study adjacent to my office and told him to stand in front of a long curtain, and as I pulled the curtain aside he saw himself in a full length mirror.

Pointing my finger at the man in the mirror I said, "There is the man who can help you. He is the *only man* who can do it, and until you become better acquainted with him and learn to depend upon him you will not find your way out of your present unfortunate condition."

He walked over closer to the mirror, looked at himself very closely as he rubbed his stubbled face, then turned to me and said, "I see what you mean, and may God bless you for not coddling me."

With that he bowed his way out and I didn't see or hear from him for almost two years when he walked in one day, so changed in appearance that I did not recognize him. He explained that he got the help of the Salvation Army in clothing himself properly. Then he got a job in a restaurant similar to the one he had formerly owned, worked in it as a headwaiter for a time when a former friend met him there by chance, heard his story and loaned him the money with which to buy the place.

He is today one of the more prosperous restaurant owners of Chicago, as rich as he needs to be in money, but richer still in having discovered the power of his own mind and how to use it as a means of contacting and drawing upon the powers of Infinite Intelligence.

TOLERANCE

When Ignorance and Superstition shall have left their last footprints on the sands of Time, it will be recorded in the book of man's crimes that his most grievous sin was that of Intolerance. The bitterest Intolerance grows out of racial and religious differences of opinion. How long, O Master of Human Destinies, until we poor mortals shall understand the folly of trying to destroy one another?

Our allotted time on this earth is but a fleeting moment, at most! Like a candle, we are lighted, shine for a few moments, and flicker out!

Why can we not so live during this earthly sojourn that when the Great Caravan called Death draws up and announces this visit about finished we shall be ready to fold our tents, and, like the Arabs of the Desert, silently follow out into the Great Unknown without fear or trembling?

I am hoping that I shall find no Jews or Gentiles, Catholics or Protestants, Germans or English, French or Russians, Whites or Blacks, when I shall have crossed the Bar to the other side.

I am hoping I shall find there only human souls, Brothers and Sisters all; unmarked by race, creed or color, so that I may lie down and rest an aeon or two, undisturbed by the petty strife and chaos and misunderstandings which too often disturb this earthly existence.

Change—the Only Permanent Thing in the Universe

THE LAW of change is one of the great miracles with which the Creator has blessed man and every other creature.

Change is an important tool in human progress. Yet, it's the one thing against which many people fight hardest. The law of change is, however, inexorable. Uncounted civilizations of Mankind have died for violating it. For the law reads that just as the physical world must undergo incessant change, Man's social and cultural world must progress or die.

But the law is a blessing. Without it, Man would still be an animal. With it he can map his own earthly destiny and create the ways and means of attaining it. It is the device by which the habits and thoughts of men continuously reshape themselves into a better system of human relations, leading toward harmony, better understanding and closer brotherhood.

You can use the law of change to achieve your individual aims of material success. Fatalism is insufficient. You must take positive steps to make events work out the way you want them, in full faith that they will come to pass if your goal is a proper one. Recognition of the law of change can ease the blows that life deals out to you. Even the loss of a loved one will be softened by acknowledgment that grief itself is something that must pass away.

Instead of resisting the law of change, make it work for you.

When Woodrow Wilson first advocated formation of the Federal Reserve System, many bankers cried out loudly against what they considered an unnecessary change from the old tried and true methods. But others, far more foresighted, knew that the old order was bound to pass away.

The result was the organization of a financial system that has saved many banks in times of emergency.

Henry Ford should have known more certainly than any man of his time that the law of change demands persistent progress. But he once lost sight of the fact—and almost lost his business.

A stubborn man, Ford refused to believe that the Model "T" could ever be supplanted despite warnings from associates.

Competitors proved him wrong and Ford's sales dropped dangerously before he realized his error and re-couped with new, modern models.

Constant repetition has not blemished the truth of the old statement that "Time and tide wait for no man." And Shakespeare said: "There is a tide in the affairs of men which, taken at the flood, leads on to fortune. Omitted, all the voyage of their life is bound in shallows and in miseries."

You must be prepared to seize the opportunities offered you by the irresistible law of change—or doom yourself to failure.

Creed For Riches

I give thanks daily, not for mere riches, but for wisdom with which to recognize, embrace, and properly use the great abundance of riches I now have at my command. I have no enemies because I injure no man for any cause, but I try to benefit all with whom I come in contact, by teaching them the way to enduring riches. I have more material wealth than I need because I am free from greed and covet only the material things I can use while I live.

INDEX BY
AUTHOR AND TITLE